The Real Red Violin

A True Story About Rembert, the "Stradivarius Wurlitzer" and *The Mendelssohn* Stradivarius, with a Play Simply Called *Rembert*

Frederick Pabst Wurlitzer

Publishing History

Paperback Black-and-White Edition 2 / July 2020
ISBN: 9798654102041

Dedication

This book is dedicated to Rembert Wurlitzer and his widow Lee. Both have now passed away.

Books by Fred Pabst Wurlitzer

The Gospel of Fred – 2019
The Second Gospel of Fred - 2019
Love to the Trinity – 2020
The Real Red Violin - 2020

Table of Contents

Foreword

While I was growing up, my father told me a number of stories about his first cousin Rembert who was my first cousin once removed. Some of these stories related to the Wurlitzer Music Company, but the most memorable story was about Rembert and a red violin. Later, I learned Rembert had authenticated and sold an amazing number of Stradivari violins.

In part, this book is a detective story attempting to identify the real red violin that became the basis for the movie *The Red Violin*. It is also a book that gives some details about Wurlitzer family history.

Mostly, this book is about a man who became totally infatuated and obsessed with rare violins.

The play in Addenda III and IV presents a story about what I think really happened around the time of Rembert's discovery of the real *Red Violin*. The play is in part a biography of an extraordinary man based on facts expanded upon by speculation.

Acknowledgements

I would like to acknowledge the grandson of Rudolph Henry Wurlitzer, William Griess, who contributed a significant number of details to this book about Wurlitzer family history, and Marianne Wurlitzer, the daughter of Rembert Wurlitzer, who added details. Mr. David Fulton provided details of the provenance of *The Mendelssohn* and the history of *La Pucelle*, a Stradivari he had owned. I give special thanks to Gabi Forbes who contributed ideas and helped with editing. Finally, I acknowledge Terry Hathaway who helped materially with editing, and Bill Smart who enabled publishing.

Introduction

This book is intended to introduce the reader to a man who authenticated and sold an amazing number of Stradivari violins. Through the auction house, Tarisio, that has an extensive record of Stradivari instruments and the *Violin Iconography of Antonio Stradivari* by Herbert Goodkind, I have determined that a Wurlitzer, mostly Rembert, handled, authenticated, and sold, most times on consignment, as many as 135 Stradivari violins, if not more. Charles Beare, who had worked with Wurlitzer, actually recalled having seen more than one-hundred Stradivari violins during his apprenticeship at Wurlitzer.[1] By some estimates, this 135 number was more than half of all known and accounted-for Stradivari violins.

Rembert had an amazingly fine and well-educated ear for Stradivari sounds. This acuity was so strong that one time he suspected an unknown, red violin was a Stradivarius by just hearing it played. To be sure, Rembert examined the instrument to confirm it was a Stradivarius.

Although many people may be familiar with the movie *The Red Violin*, they are unlikely to know the factually-based story behind it.

---

[1] Freddie Beare reported this to Mr. David Fulton

As this story forms part of my own family's oral history, I felt it was worth investigating and documenting in order to share with others.

This book is about one of the greatest dealers ever of Stradivari violins. Rembert was a remarkable man unusually enthusiastic and knowledgeable about Stradivari instruments and, in particular, Stradivari violins.

Finally, this book is a detective story trying to determine what Stradivari violin known to collectors today is really the *Red Violin*.

The Real Red Violin
A True Story About

Rembert, the "Stradivarius Wurlitzer"

The man who came from a family making musical instruments for about 400 years,
The man who sold more authenticated Stradivari violins than anyone else ever,
The man who doubtless discovered the famous *Mendelssohn* violin of legend,
The man who for decades was the world's authority on Stradivari violins,
The man who for decades was the authority on Stradivari instruments,
This man may have traded over half of all known Strad violins.
This man is a principal in a mystery story about a red violin;
This man was "The Resurrector of The Mendelssohn."

By Frederick Pabst Wurlitzer

Rembert Wurlitzer

Farny Wurlitzer (1883–1972), my great uncle and CEO of The Wurlitzer Company years after my grandfather, Howard Wurlitzer (1871–1928) died, traced with the help of my great uncle Rudolph Henry Wurlitzer (1873–1948), a family tree back to the ancient Teutonic knights' family of Wurr of Nürnberg or Nuremberg, around 1000 C.E.

Years afer my grandfather Howard Wurlitzer died in 1928, my great uncle Farny Wurlitzer, who later becaame CEO of the Wurlitzer company, resolved to trace the family tree together with my great uncle Rudolph. Their research established a trail all the way back to the Teutonic knights of 1000 C.E., through a family named Wurr of Nurnberg or Nuremberg. My personal DNA analysis suggests a Viking ancestry.

There is no record of music-making among the Wurr family. "*Itz*," in old German, may have meant "a place," like "*plätz*" and "*er*" probably meant "from," so the "*Wurlitzers*" were from places where the family named "Wurr" had lived.

The old Wurr knights and early Wurlitzers had a beautifully distinctive coat of arms. On the back of this painting below of the family coat of arms that Farny gave me years ago, he wrote the family tree. Wurlitzers first started making musical instruments about 400 years ago.

A painting commissioned by Farny Wurlitzer

On July 6, 1964, Farny gave an address to the American Association of Theatre Organ Enthusiasts (ATOE)[2] in Buffalo, New York. Farny traced the family tree again, as he had done on the back of the coat of arms painting. The first Wurlitzer, after the Wurr's, was Heinrich Wurlitzer born in 1596, and then Nicolaus Wurlitzer, born in 1659, who made musical instruments. Heinrich probably made musical instruments before Nicolaus, although that is not recorded.

In John H. Fairfield's, *Known Violin Makers*, published in New York in 1942, and adding to the Wurlitzer family tree, Mr. Fairfield states that John George Wurlitzer, who was born in 1726, followed the craft of violin making. Hans Adam Wurlitzer was elected in 1701 to membership in the lute makers' guild of Saxony, and in 1732 he was identified as a master violin maker.[3] There were other Wurlitzer music makers besides Nicolaus, John, and Hans. Another member of the family, Frederick Wurlitzer, my namesake, was a child musical prodigy who toured Europe in concert presentations and became the court pianist to Frederick the Great of Prussia at the age of sixteen.

[2] https://www.atos.org/wurlitzer-company.
[3] Presto-Times, Page 9, May-June 1933.

From father to oldest son following primogeniture, and sometimes younger sons, Wurlitzer music craftsmanship, musical instrument sales, and performing took place over four centuries. Making musical instruments was a home business. In East Germany, the name "Wurlitzer" became a word synonymous with a musical instrument maker or someone involved somehow with music.

About 30 years ago when I visited Schöneck ("beautiful corner") in East Germany, the home of Franz Rudolph Wurlitzer, founder of the Wurlitzer Company, I saw musical instruments over 200 years old with the name of Wurlitzer on them in the nearby museum, the Musikinstrumenten-Museum Markneukirchen in Saxony. The story of Wurlitzers making musical instruments including violins as "*Geigenbaumeisters*" (i.e., expert violin makers) starting about 400 years ago is a remarkable one. Although I was trained as a surgical oncologist, I remain intrigued by Wurlitzer history.

When I was a boy, my father, Raimund Wurlitzer (1896 – 1986) who was the only son of Franz Rudolph Wurlitzer's eldest son Howard Wurlitzer, told me many stories about the Wurlitzer Music Company and in particular stories about Rembert Wurlitzer (1904 – 1963), his first cousin and my first cousin once removed who discovered a red Stradivarius violin.

Rembert was born in Cincinnati as the only son of Rudolph Henry Wurlitzer (1873–1948), who, in turn, was the second son of Franz Rudolph Wurlitzer (1831–1914). In 1856, after emigrating from Schöneck in 1853, Franz Rudolph founded the Rudolph Wurlitzer Company that is usually referred to as simply "Wurlitzer" or the "Wurlitzer Music Company" that came to be listed on the NYSE.[4] [5]

---

[4] https://en.wikipedia.org/wiki/Wurlitzer.
[5] Although Wikipedia states Rudolph Wurlitzer founded his company in 1853, that date is incorrect. Rudolph arrived on the Adolphine from Bremen in June 1853. After working for other people for about three years, he actually started his company the Rudolph Wurlitzer Company in 1856.

One time, my father told me that at a Wurlitzer Board meeting, a discussion arose about what to name Wurlitzer player-piano rolls. My grandfather, Howard, the CEO, suggested "ABC" rolls. My father suggested a more original name, "QRS," and so Wurlitzer piano rolls became "QRS rolls" at my father's suggestion. This may not seem like a very big deal, but it is for many theater organ society members.

Other stories followed, but this is not the place to recount them. It astounds me that among American Theatre Organ Society members and other organ society members worldwide, there is such fascination with Wurlitzer family history.

After working with Wurlitzer, Rembert dropped out of Princeton so he could become more of an authority on rare violins. After studying violins and violin-making in Mirecourt, France, in Italy and Germany, and then in England for two and a half years,[6] studying under the then-leading violin expert of the world, Alfred Hill and later his dad, Rudolph Henry, his father finally considered him an authority on rare violins.

Alfred Hill was so impressed with the young Rembert that he asked him to join W.E. Hill & Sons, but Rembert respectfully declined. He worked instead at the "Wurlitzer violin finishing school" learning a great deal more from his dad, Rudolph Henry, who had studied violins in Berlin. Rembert also learned shop skills from many violin dealers he visited.

In 1926, the Wurlitzer board considered him ready at the age of 22, to be in charge of acquisitions for the Wurlitzer Violin Department.[7] For twenty-three years, Rembert bought, authenticated and sold, often on consignment, Stradivari instruments aggressively.

---

[6] Cited by William Griess, grandson of Rudolph Henry Wurlitzer
[7] Music Trades, Page 13, December 25, 1926.

In 1949, he formed the Rembert Wurlitzer Company.[8] Over time, Rembert developed an obsessive and possessive interest in Stradivari violins, increasing his unusually insightful knowledge through his ever-growing rare violin purchasing experiences.

My favorite story that I heard several times from my father was how Rembert discovered a Stradivarius violin. He was sitting at an outside café in Berlin with my father when a gentleman whom Rembert presumed to be a gypsy started playing a violin – a red violin. Rembert perked up, and then after listening intently, he said to his companions and my father, "That violin may be a Stradivarius." His examination of the violin confirmed it was a Stradivarius.

This story seemed to me as a youth interesting but not world-shaking. My father's narration, which was not the least bit hearsay, was direct confirmation of how Rembert discovered a red Stradivarius violin. This Rembert red violin was, in my opinion, almost certainly the legendary *Mendelssohn*.

One can reasonably speculate that Rembert's appointment to be in charge of Wurlitzer acquisitions in 1926 was in part to make sure he did not work for W.H. Hill who had offered him a job. Secondly, one can assume the Wurlitzer Board was impressed with Rembert's discovery of a rare, red Stradivarius violin. Rembert's knowledge and expertise was very apparent. His find of a rare, red violin surely impressed the Board enough for them to consider making him their master of acquisitions, according to my father. Time would prove their assessment to be well founded.

---

[8] *Wurlitzer Family History* by Lloyd Graham 1955 in the "Second-Generation" chapter and *New York Herald Tribune* Obituary October 22, 1953.

Rembert Wurlitzer (1904–1963)
Probably in the late 1920s

Although Walter Hamma (1916–1988), a German violin maker and dealer, surely visited Berlin from time to time, I suspect it was not often because his business was in Stuttgart. It was not Hamma who discovered the red violin in Berlin, I claim, although Tarisio lists him as the first recorded owner of The Mendelssohn (Tarisio #40316) and Rembert as the second recorded owner after Lilli and Franz von Mendelssohn followed by Joseph Joachim. Tarisio does not list Joachim as a later owner.[9]

It was certainly a coincidence that Rembert, one of the world's greatest authorities on Stradivari instruments, happened to be present when someone played an unknown Stradivari. It was well known that Rembert had a very good ear.

Who actually discovered *The (Red) Mendelssohn*, I do not definitively know, except in my opinion, it was not Walter Hamma, but rather Rembert. If I knew which red violin for sure, I might cheekily call it the *"Rembert Red Stradivarius,"* if it was not *The*

---

[9] https://tarisio.com/cozio-archive/property/?ID=40316.

Mendelssohn, because Rembert discovered a red Stradivarius. There are few Stradivari violins as red as *The Mendelssohn*. By a process of elimination and other evidence that will be presented, the red Stradivarius Rembert discovered was likely *The Mendelssohn*.

Another suspect that is about as red in color as *The Mendelssohn* is a Stradivari violin Tarisio #51374, I call the *"Unnamed,"* whose provenance began with Rembert. Tarisio does not list any earlier owners than Rembert, so who owned this violin before Rembert? It may be just a coincidence that *The Unnamed* and *The Mendelssohn* were both made in 1720. If this unnamed violin is the one Rembert discovered in Berlin at an outdoor cafe, I would rename it also the *"Rembert Red Stradivarius"* in order to be consistent in giving Rembert credit. My prime suspect remains, however, *The Mendelssohn*. It would be interesting indeed if both Tarisio #51374 and #40316 could be shown to be the same violin, *The Mendelssohn*.

Others have also speculated that the red violin discovered by Rembert was undeniably the *"Red Mendelssohn of 1720"* or just *"The Mendelssohn"* that inspired the movie, *The Red Violin*. Rembert did purchase *The Mendelssohn* in 1956 according to Tarisio, well after selling it, I suspect, to Hamma in Stuttgart in the mid- to late-1920s. My best guess is that the year was 1926 before Rembert was appointed head of Wurlitzer acquisitions.

My surmise is that Rembert did not enter his purchase of *The Mendelssohn* in 1956 into his inventory, because the violin was a "keeper" holding special meaning to him. Nonetheless, Freddie Beare, whose father worked for Wurlitzer, wrote in a private email in July 2020, "I've done some digging in the Wurlitzer database and found an instrument that matches the "*Mendelssohn*." Mr. Beare may be correct. If his supposition is incorrect, my surmise is that Rembert purposely kept the violin out of inventory of instruments meant to be sold. The violin was a keeper as much as his wedding ring, never to be sold.

Admittedly, this rationale for not listing the violin is speculation, but it is speculation based on history as presented in the play that follows called simply *Rembert*.

There is a tendency among dealers to strongly discredit Tarisio records. Although there are certainly many inconsistencies in Tarisio records, there are also many truths. So, when Tarisio lists violins #40316 and #51374 Stradivari of 1720 as being owned by Rembert, or at least consigned to Rembert, I find their assertions interesting and more than consistent with my father's story that Rembert found a red Stradivarius in Berlin.

As Mr. Fulton pointed out in a private email, there is no accurate way by examination of known records to prove or disprove Rembert found *The Mendelssohn*. My claim is that Rembert did find *The Mendelssohn*. The play develops that claim.

Hamma records are unavailable, at least to me, because his company is out of business. On my behalf, Friedericke Philipson of the Musikinstrumenten-Museum in Markneukirchen, near the ancestral home of Schöneck, contacted Hans Rehberg in Freudenstadt Obermusbach, who has researched the Hamma Family.

Unfortunately, Mr. Rehberg does not know where the documents of the company went and so could not be of help either in tracking down the history of *The Mendelssohn* further. Marianne Wurlitzer, the daughter of Rembert, could not be of help either. So, in part, this story of a Rembert red violin remains a mystery.

Walter Hamma working on a violin, possibly in the 1920s.
Walter Hamma was a colleague of Rembert

Mr. David Fulton is probably the greatest collector of rare musical instruments today. He has a copy of Rembert's database and unusual access to information about rare musical instruments. Mr. Fulton provided a provenance attached at the end of this book and play of *The Mendelssohn*.

The first recorded owner of *The Mendelssohn*, according to the Fulton provenance, is a Sig. Bernardo Darhan, sometime around 1850 or 1860. Then there is Francesco Mendelssohn in 1913 followed by Elizabeth Pitcairn in 1990. It is the intent of this book, in large part, to fill in the gaps from 1913 to 1990.

Filling in the gaps conclusively is not possible at this time. Mr. Fulton suggests Francesco Mendelssohn sold *The Mendelssohn* to Français, followed by Fred Smith, Rosenthal, and Max Verabay. In my opinion, there were other intermediaries including Rembert. The provenance after Francesco Mendelssohn is incomplete.

Rembert bought *The Mendelssohn* in 1956 from Hamma, according to Tarisio #40316, and then sometime after 1956 and before his death in 1963, Rembert (or, if after 1963, his wife, Lee) sold *The Mendelssohn* to Luther Rosenthal and son.[10]

Although there is currently no irrefutable evidence that *The Mendelssohn* was the violin that Rembert discovered before Hamma obtained the violin, there is circumstantial evidence, namely the story my father told me about it being red in color – and there is still other evidence including the Tarisio accountings. Evidence that Rembert found *The Mendelssohn* will be developed more fully.

There is also a gap of about forty years in provenance from the time of Felix Mendelssohn (1809-1847) to Sig. Bernando Darhan's ownership. When Rembert discovered the violin, there was a remarkable 100-year more-or-less gap. Rembert did not call the violin *The Mendelssohn*. He didn't know the history, and at the time he was not working for Wurlitzer. It was his violin. It did not have to be entered into Wurlitzer inventory. -It was an unnamed Stradivarius Tarisio records as #51374. If that violin can be shown to be *The Mendelssohn*, the provenance becomes more complete.

An unusual and very entertaining character in the provenance history of *The Mendelssohn* was the great nephew of Felix, Francesco Mendelssohn, who died in 1971. There is little doubt Francesco owned his namesake violin in 1913.

Rembert knew him very well, so well in fact that he lent Francesco a violin he had made in Mirecourt many years earlier. He pleaded with Francesco not to take his Stradivarius cello, *The Piatti,* with him on a trip. Francesco listened, fortunately, because a fire occurred in the dwelling where Francesco was staying and

---

[10] https://tarisio.com/cozio-archive/property/?ID=40316.

Rembert's violin was destroyed. A very valuable Stradivarius was saved. I wonder whether or not it was a drunken stupor that Francesco had which caused him to accidentally set the fire.

Francesco was a confirmed alcoholic fond of drunken torpors. He had a habit of leaving his *Piatti* in bars as assurance for paying bar bills later. One night after a concert (he was an expert cellist), Francesco tried to enter his home on East 62nd St. in New York. Awakening to the fact, despite being in an alcoholic stupor, that he was at the wrong house, he left his cello on the footpath as he staggered off to his own home. The next morning, the housekeeper awoke him and asked if a cello she had found on the street was his. "I found it on the street just as a garbage truck was about to pick it up."[11] Who could make up a story like that? Truth was more entertaining than fiction.

In the play that follows, I speculate that Francesco had a similar episode in Berlin when he left *The Mendelssohn* on a street after a drunken evening. That time a garbage truck picked up the violin and sold it to a gypsy who in 1926 played the Stradivarius at an outside Berlin bar. Francesco didn't report the loss to Berlin authorities, I surmise, because he was a Jew.

When I met Rembert three times in Manhattan with my father when I was a lad, I wish I had asked him which violin my father said he had discovered. I wish my father had asked too, but the movie *The Red Violin* was yet to be made. *The Red Violin* name had little, if any meaning to me, my father, or possibly even Rembert back then, although in my immediate Wurlitzer household lore there had been a red violin that Rembert had discovered.

Wurlitzer became a leading international center for rare string instruments under Rudolph Henry, Rembert's father. It bought, held on consignment, sold, authenticated, and/or restored

---

[11] https://www.irishtimes.com/culture/memoirs-of-a-stradivarius-1.932980

more than half the world's 600 known Stradivari (not all violins), and supplied instruments to Fritz Kreisler, David Oistrakh, and Isaac Stern, among others.[12] Wurlitzer's rare violin acquisitions were independently directed by Rembert after 1926.

In 1949, Rembert founded the Rembert Wurlitzer Company after buying out the Wurlitzer rare violin department. Rembert handled a host of other important old, rare musical instruments including Guadagninis, Amatis, del Gesùs, Gaglianos, Roccas. Bergonzis, Stainers, Lorenzinis, Guarneris, and Giuseppes.

Much ado has been made that Rembert was not a collector. But there is indisputable evidence that after his death in 1949, there was an extensive inventory, not entirely on consignment, including the *Hellier* Stradivarius that his widow Lee held.[13] Moreover, during his career at Wurlitzer from 1926 to 1949, he purchased on behalf of Wurlitzer an impressive collection of rare musical instruments.

---

[12] https://en.wikipedia.org/wiki/Rembert_Wurlitzer_Co.
[13] https://www.nytimes.com/1974/08/13/archives/wurlitzer-to-shut-down-oldinstrument-concern.html

Rudolph Henry is shown in the Wurlitzer Old Violin Room in 1906.

Rembert learned a great amount from his dad.

Over the course of many years, a Wurlitzer handled and/or sold, mostly on consignment, 135 or more Stradivari violins. Rudolph Henry or Wurlitzer, led by Rembert's rare violin purchasing, bought and sold, some on consignment, about thirty-nine of these 135.

Rembert sold the rest independently after 1949 through the Rembert Wurlitzer Company. Goodkind often lists Wurlitzer as owner, consignee, or the seller as "Wurlitzer" without differentiating between Rembert and Rudolph or the ownership structure. Dealers such as W.H. Hill and Hamma may have handled as many rare instruments as Rembert or Wurlitzer, but their records are unavailable. It was never my intent to compare numbers of rare musical instruments various dealers handled.

Stradivari Violins

"It is estimated that in total, Antonio Stradivari made around 1,100 musical instruments in total. This total is probably exaggerated according to Beare and Fulton. Of these, 600 (not all violins) are still thought to be in existence. Of that number, one source states only 244 violins are currently accounted for."[14] Wikipedia lists 248 known Stradivari violins.[15] Goodkind lists 635 Stradivari violins.[16] Most of these numbers are probably misleading. Estimates of known and accounted for Stradivari violins are widely inconsistent. The Goodkind number of 635 may be the most accurate.

The definitive work on Stradivari violins is the *Violin Iconography of Antonio Stradivari* by Herbert Goodkind who lists 635 Stradivari violins known but not necessarily accounted for entirely at the time of writing. This number is profoundly different from the estimates of 244 to 248 Wikipedia and other sources represent as being accounted for. E. Doring lists 440 known Strads and W.E. Hill 175. Mr. Goodkind's estimate of 635 is probably a more accurate figure, although a number of the Strads he lists have sketchy provenances. Mr. Goodkind estimates that about 2,000 Stradivari

---

[14] https://newviolinist.com/how-many-stradivarius-violins-are-there/.
[15] https://en.wikipedia.org/wiki/List_of_Stradivarius_instruments.
[16] Goodkind, Herbert. Violin Iconography of Antonio Stradivari. 1972 Self-published by Larchmont, New York.

instruments were originally made, and of these, about 800 original Stradivari violins.

At least 135 of all the known Antonio Stradivari violins in the world were held mostly on consignment at one time or another by Rembert or Wurlitzer where Rembert had been in charge of violin sales and purchases after 1926. Rudolph is credited with up to thirty-nine of the 135, even though most of the early Wurlitzer purchases were at the direction of Rembert after 1926, so almost all of the Stradivari violins handled or sold, mostly on consignment, by a Wurlitzer were by Rembert.

Nine violins of this 135 number were made by Francesco and Omobono Stradivari, who were sons of Antonio. Technically, these nine were Stradivari, but not Antonio Stradivaris.

Depending upon which number of Stradivari one accepts as being known and accounted for, Rembert handled, authenticated, held on consignment and then sold anywhere from 22% to 56%, that is possibly over half of all known Stradivari violins accounted for in this world. Records are so diverse and different, it is more than likely Wurlitzers handled or held on consignment more than 136 Stradivari violins.

These facts may confirm Rembert had been one of the world's foremost rare violin authority and owner or consignee of the most Stradivari violins during his era. Hamma or W.H. Hill may have dealt with more rare musical instruments, but it is not my intent to compare numbers.

A list of the violins so far identified as having been handled or held by Wurlitzer (a.k.a. the Rudolph Wurlitzer Company or Wurlitzer Music Company) or Rembert is shown in Appendix I. This list may still be incomplete. As my research continues, I would not be surprised to identify more.

This brief study is a story of Rembert and the Stradivari that he loved and, in particular, *The Mendelssohn* of 1720 that he had owned and that violinist Elizabeth Pitcairn now owns. Among my personal memories, I refer to Rembert as the "Stradivarius Wurlitzer" just as there was a "Clarinet Wurlitzer" whom I met in East Germany and whose family, including Fritz and Herman historically, still makes clarinets today.[17] Furthermore, I respectfully suggest that *The Mendelssohn* of 1720 is the Red Violin my father told me about several times when I was a youth well before the movie *The Red Violin* ever emerged. My father was not an expert in violins, but he had a fantastic memory. If the two red Stradivari of 1920 (Tarisio #40316 and #51374) are ever shown to be the same violin, namely *The Mendelssohn*, the evidence would be almost irrefutable it was *The Mendelssohn* that Rembert found.

I have little doubt that when Rembert discovered his red Stradivarius, he did not know the provenance. It was only later after he researched it that the provenance became better known or suspected. It must have been very difficult for Rembert to certify alone the red violin as a Stradivari that had a 100-year or so gap in provenance. He may have called on his dad, Rudolph, for help, but there is no correspondence between them available to confirm this speculation.

In the play *Rembert* that follows in Addenda III and IV, Rudolph plays a material role in confirming the red violin Rembert found was a Stradivarius. His widow Lee, who took over management of the Rembert Wurlitzer company after he died in 1963, is no longer alive to confirm the time line presented in the play.

---

[17] https://wurlitzerklarinetten.de/clarinets/?lang=en.

While the provenance was still incomplete, records somewhere had shown *The Mendelssohn*, and Joseph Joachim had owned it.[18] Rembert and his dad were good detectives when searching for the history of a rare musical instrument. At the time, there was little reason to publicize the discovery, and moreover, Rembert did not seek publicity. The red violin was, after all, just another Stradivarius, and Wurlitzer had owned or dealt with many.

The violin's provenance was certainly not immediately known. Circumstantial evidence, based primarily on my father's story and the deep, red color fairly uncommon[19] among rare Stradivari violins, and Tarisio renditions is that the red violin was *The Mendelssohn* and that the discoverer and authenticator was Rembert, possibly with the help of his dad, Rudolph Henry, also an authority on rare violins. Anthony Zatorski, speaking for Tarisio, informed me that they did not have the Rembert authentications that might have been of help in identifying the suspect violins and their histories further.

Before Walter Hamma obtained the violin, he would certainly have required authentication, and there was no one better qualified than Rembert to have provided authentication. In the rare-violin sales business, Rembert was truly an independent expert in the late 1920s to 1930s, and for many decades later.

Although those who sold violins usually authenticated them, many authentications were false, because few dealers except for Rembert or Rudolph, and of course W.H. Hill and Hamma, were completely honest or had the knowledge and experience to determine authenticity accurately. It took a good ear too to confirm the authenticity of a Stradivarius sound.

Violins have been forged for generations. Violin forgery in the

---

[18] The Pitcairn website cites Joachim as having owned *The Mendelssohn*.
　　Marianne Wurlitzer and Mr. Fulton doubt Joachim owned *The Mendelssohn*.
[19] The violins *Ruby Strad* and *The Sassoon* are also red Stradivari.

nineteenth century was an industry for hundreds of luthiers. Few individuals had the skills and ear necessary to determine if a so-called rare violin, specifically a Stradivari, was genuine. Rembert had those talents. So did Alfred Hill, Charles Beare and Robert Bein.

According to Fulton, "Strads are so well-made that they are virtually impossible to forge. That is not the case with del Gesù. There are many forgeries of del Gesù." That is not to say that there are not many crude forgeries of both Strads and del Gesùs

Authentications from Rembert, whose integrity was untarnished and almost unmatched, were genuine, and so Rembert's (and Rudolph's) authentication would have been almost certainly necessary before Hamma bought an expensive Stradivari and especially a Stradivari violin with a 100-year gap in known ownership. The resurrection of an unknown Stradivari violin with a 100-year breach in history undoubtedly aroused profound suspicion that it was a fake. These particulars give circumstantial weight to the argument that Rembert was involved with *The Mendelssohn* before Hamma obtained it – probably from Rembert himself.

Hamma would have been a fool to not have involved Rembert and Rudolph. Besides, who else would have been reliable authenticators? The Hills, well-known English, rare-violin dealers, did not speak fluent German, and Walter Hamma's first language was German. Rudolph spoke fluent German as his first language, and he and other Wurlitzers had long-time relationships with Hamma. Moreover, the Hills were, according to some commentator,s anti-anything not English and anti-semetic. Hamma was Jewish.

The 100-year-or-so gap in provenance was unique, because Stradivari instruments are so well known and prized. Yet, scores of Stradivari violins remain lost or unaccounted for. *The Mendelssohn* had simply disappeared for about 100 years, only to be resurrected sometime, probably in the mid- to late-1920s. My best guess was in 1926. This 100-year gap is part of this mystery story. Now through extensive research, there are fewer gaps.

Henceforth, I am respectfully also calling Rembert, "The Resurrector of *The Mendelssohn*." After Rembert's clearly recorded ownership in 1956, according to Tarisio, immediately after Hanna's, he "resurrected" the violin again seeking to confirm who had owned the violin earlier. Until then, *The Mendelssohn* may have had another name in Rembert's inventory, since his daughter Marianne does not recall that a violin called *The Mendelssohn* was in the inventory when she worked with her mother Lee after Rembert died.

Alternatively, Rembert may not have entered *The Mendelssohn* into his own inventory. Still, there is little doubt based upon Tarisio confirmations and other evidence that he had owned it. Rembert would have seen his red violin as a "keeper," a special entity in his existence.

Violins entered into inventories were meant to be sold. I suggest Rembert did not want his red violin entered into inventory, because he had no intentions of selling it, ever.

The timeline for Rembert's discovery suggests it was between 1925 and 1928. The violin may have been entered briefly into the Wurlitzer inventory, but I doubt that too because at the time of discovery, he was not working for Wurlitzer. If there was an entry in Wurlitzer inventory, and that inventory was recovered, there would be a date. He did not start working for Wurlitzer until 1926. My best guess is that he found his red violin shortly before working for Wurlitzer. I remain absolutely convinced that Rembert did indeed find a red violin because of what my father told me. The incident almost certainly took place in the 1920s before my father left Wurlitzer in 1928.

Lee has since passed on, and Wurlitzer records relating to *The Mendelssohn* are not helpful, as recalled by Marianne or Goodkind. But Tariso records confirm Wurlitzer or Rembert had owned at least two Stradivari violins of 1720, at least one or both of them being *The Mendelssohn*.

Goodkind lists four Stradivari violins of 1720 that a Wurlitzer had owned or sold on consignment. Goodkind's records included

Rembert's records passed on to Goodkind by Marianne, the daughter of Rembert. These Stradivari violins were *The Bishop* or *Leveque*, the *Madrileno*, the *Bavarian*, and *The Woolhouse*. Goodkind does not list a Wurlitzer as having owned or sold *The Mendelssohn*. Clearly, Goodkind does not support any relationship between a Wurlitzer and *The Mendelssohn*. So, how could Goodkind and Marianne have been wrong?

The Wurlitzer Music Company inventory is unavailable today, despite my best efforts to locate it. Goodkind did not have access to all the Wurlitzer Music Company inventory. It is possible Rembert took the red Stradivarius back to America, put it in Wurlitzer inventory, and then Wurlitzer later sold it privately to Hamma around 1926 or later even in the 1930s without the red violin ever being in Rembert's or Goodkind's later inventory and iconography. I do not believe that scenario is likely.

In the play that follows, I relate what I think really happened without having total factual support. I suggest strongly Rembert never entered the red violin into his later Rembert Wurlitzer inventory because it was a "keeper," an instrument that held tremendous emotional value for him. Items entered into inventory were meant to be sold, and he did not want to sell his red violin. Ask yourself how likely it would be for your mother (or wife if, you are a man) to sell her wedding ring?

Elizabeth Pitcairn, the current owner of *The Mendelssohn,* is alleged to view her violin as "her life's most inspiring mentor and friend."[20] I respectfully and strongly suspect Rembert viewed the same violin with similar feelings.

Among the violins the Rembert Wurlitzer Co. owned and then sold was the Henry Hottinger Collection bought in 1967. About thirty violins in all (not all were Stradivari) from that collection were

---

[20] Suzanne Marcus Fletcher alleged this in a program for a performance by Pitcairn with The Mendelssohn.

subsequently dispersed all over the world. Additionally, there was Rudolph Wurlitzer Company's 1929 purchase of the famous Wanamaker Collection of forty-four stringed instruments that was at the time the finest collection of Stradivari, Amati, and other old violins in the world.

On September 20, 1953, Rembert temporarily loaned four Stradivari instruments to the La Salle String Quartet so their musicians could play them at a Cincinnati College of Music performance supported by my grandmother, Helene Wurlitzer. According to William Griess, a grandson of Rudolph Henry Wurlitzer (1873 – 1948), "These were the *Baron Knoop* violin of 1715, the *Medici* viola of 1690, the *La Pucelle* violin of 1709 and the *Davidoff* cello of 1712." William Griess, whose parents kept the program for this performance, represented to me these four instruments were used.

That event later confirmed by Mr. Fulton, a previous owner, that Rembert had on consignment, at one time *La Pucelle,* or *"The Virgin."* Mr. David L. Fulton of Seattle has probably the largest collection today of rare musical instruments.[21] The Tarisio Auction house, in its index of rare violins, does not cite Rembert as a past owner or a consignee of *The Virgin.* Nor does Goodkind. That absence is a mistake, in my opinion, and is representative of the frequent difficulty interpreting inventory lists and records.

David Fulton confirmed recently in private correspondence that Rembert had *La Pucelle* on consignment in 1953 from Mr. Frank Otwell. "Finally, on 5/11/55, Wurlitzers purchased the fiddle from consignment. It's fun to note that Wurlitzer bought the fiddle for $25,000 while the consignment had been for $42,000." Mr. Otwell was apparently eager to sell the fiddle. When Mr. Fulton's foundation sold the fiddle in 2019, it fetched $22 million. All may agree that was an impressive financial appreciation.

---

[21] https://en.wikipedia.org/wiki/David_L._Fulton.

Mr. Fulton confirms Rembert had on consignment the other quartet instruments loaned to La Salle. Rembert was a man of great integrity, and even if instruments were on consignment, he would not have exposed them to unnecessary misadventure.

Violins sold and authenticated by Wurlitzer retained a "Wurlitzer Number," a number glued inside the fiddle. Rembert put it in there so he could later identify the instruments. According to David Fulton, "The Wurlitzers always did that; the Hills always did that. Bein and Fushi also did that." [22]

The Wurlitzer stock cards reveal a great deal about an instrument. They would put on the stock card the history of the instrument as it passed through their hands, as well as what they paid and sold it for in a code. They encoded it so that someone glancing at the stock card couldn't necessarily tell what it sold for."[23] But Fulton knows the secret.

Mr. Fulton, with his database of Rembert records, was of help expanding the history of *The Mendelssohn*. Gaps still remained. He was of great help expanding the provenance of *La Pucelle of 1709*.

A resource used in this book, in addition to the Wikipedia list of Stradivari instruments, is the book *Stradivari* by Stewart Pollens. And still another resource is the previously mentioned, very expensive and exhaustive *Violin Iconography of Antonio Stradivari 1644-1737* with treatises on the life and work of the "Patriarch" of violinmakers including an inventory of 700 known or recorded Stradivari string instruments and an index of 3,500 names of past or present Stradivari owners and photographs of 400 Stradivari instruments with 1,500 views in cloth in a slipcase. This book was inscribed by Herbert K. Goodkind as a paperback in 1972. Goodkind's book is undoubtedly the most authoritative work today on Stradivari violins, and its

---

[22] Visiting David Fulton, collector of Strads, del Gesù and more.
    https://www.violinist.com/blog/laurie/20175/21182/
[23] https://en.wikipedia.org/wiki/David_L._Fulton delete gap.

inventory is far more extensive than the Tarisio database. My copy is autographed by Goodkind. A third resource was William Griess, grandson of Rudolph Henry Wurlitzer, who confirmed that the La Salle String Quartet performance program showed four instruments were made available by Rembert on September 20, 1953. Mr. Griess made a copy available to me of the Farny address in 1964 and reviewed this study as to its accuracy. A fourth source was Terry Hathaway, whose domain has been automatic musical instruments. Terry, who is an expert on Wurlitzer family history, reviewed this work also. A fifth source was the auction house Tarisio with their database taken off the Internet. A sixth, a particularly valuable resource, was Friederike Philipson from the Musikinstrumenten – the Museum Markneukirchen, who provided early photographs of Wurlitzers. She also confirmed Hamma's records were unavailable or no longer in existence. A seventh resource was Marianne Wurlitzer, the daughter of Rembert.

These principal resources collectively confirm the number of known Stradivari violins to be at least 248 and up to 635, and that Rembert or Wurlitzer handled and/or sold, mostly on consignment, 135 or more Stradivari violins at one time or another. The profound difference in numbers of Stradivari violins known and accounted for is indeed disturbing, but these differences are indisputable.

Goodkind's inventory is probably the most accurate, although it has errors as well, to wit, not listing Rembert being connected with the *La Pucelle of 1709* that he loaned to the La Salle String Quartet. There are other errors as well including those relating to *The Mendelssohn*.

As to who was one of the greatest collectors ever, it was Rembert, although he did not own all his Stradivari violins at the same time. Even Count Ignazio Alessandro Cozio di Salabue, often referred to as the supreme collector of violins, had only ten Stradivari violins,[24] and Luigi Tarisio who died in 1854 had twenty-four Stradivari violins in

---

[24] https://en.wikipedia.org/wiki/Ignazio_Alessandro_Cozio_di_Salabue.

his estate after his death.[25] But dealers such as Hamma and W.H. Hills may have handled more violins than Rembert. I doubt anyone will ever know for sure.

The greatest collector today is Mr. Fulton. "Over the years he has owned eight Strads, eight del Gesù, and 14 other instruments (violins, violas and cellos) with names such as Bergonzi, Guadagnini, Amati, Rugeri, Montagnana and Testore." [26]

The list at the end of this paper in Appendix I shows the breakdown from these sources of the Stradivari violins handled or held on consignment at different times by Rembert himself and by him and his dad Rudolph for the Wurlitzer Co. It has been difficult to develop a full list of Stradivari violins owned or on consignment at one time or another by Rembert, even using multiple resources, because so many records are incomplete, inaccurate, or unconsolidated, and sometimes differ from each other profoundly. It has been difficult to develop a case identifying unequivocally the red Stradivarius Rembert found probably in the late 1920s when my father was present.

After much research, I suspect Rembert or Wurlitzer owned or had on consignment at one time or another more than 135 Stradivari violins, including *La Pucelle*. After all, no one, a hundred years ago, I more than suspect, was so compulsive that records had to be always complete any more than an artist might compulsively keep track of all his or her paintings. Certainly, there are significant differences between Tarisio's and Goodkind's records and records compiled by other experts such as the Hammas', Henley, Hill, and Doring.[27] In fact, there is almost as much inconsistency as consistency.

---

[25] https://en.wikipedia.org/wiki/Luigi_Tarisio.
[26] Visiting David Fulton, collector of Strads, del Gesù and more.
     https://www.violinist.com/blog/laurie/20175/21182/
[27] Goodkind, H.K. *Violin Iconography of Antonio Stradivari*. Page 14.

In compiling the list of violins handled by Rembert based on the provenances provided by Tarisio Auction house, caution is warranted. Tarisio is named after the great violin collector, Luigi Tarisio, who died in 1854. After his death, the famous luthier and master violin forger, Jean-Baptiste Vuillaume, found 144 violins, including twenty-four Stradivaris, in Luigi's attic.[28] Unfortunately, Luigi kept no records of any of his transactions, nor inventory of his collections. The auction house Tarisio now provides old provenances for many of the Tarisio/Vuillaume violins. Recent transactions and provenances of Stradivari violins are now better recorded including ownership by Rembert, but even Rembert's records as recorded by Goodkind when referencing old provenances are not infallible.[29]

Identifying Stradivari forgeries is not easy or a totally trustworthy skill any more than identifying old master painting forgeries. On an often-cited occasion, Vuillaume made two copies of Paganini's Guarneri *"del Gesù," Il Cannone*. Paganini could not identify among the three violins his original *"del Gesù"* by craftsmanship or by sound.[30] Vuillaume made copies of *The Messiah*, and today there is widespread speculation that *The Messiah* in the Ashmolean Museum of Art and Archaeology in Oxford is a Vuillaume forgery.[31] Even experts like W. Hill, Rudolph, or Rembert undoubtedly made mistakes in authentication that were sometimes left unrecorded, or better yet, corrected later.

Unfortunately, mistakes had become not unheard of at Wurlitzer, but only rarely with Rembert who corrected mistakes by others. One reason why Rembert separated from Wurlitzer was a significant

---

[28] https://en.wikipedia.org/wiki/Luigi_Tarisio.
[29] https://tarisio.com/cozio-archive/cozio-carteggio/luigi-tarisio-part-1; and part 2.
[30] https://en.wikipedia.org/wiki/Il_Cannone_Guarnerius.
[31] The "widespread speculation" may be grandstanding by Stuart Pollens.

problem from outstanding guarantees on discredited instruments from one employee in particular who had been head of the rare instrument department, curator of the Wurlitzer collection and in charge of repairs, but not authentications. In forming the Rembert Wurlitzer Company in 1949, Rembert was quoted as saying he "didn't want to spend the rest of his life buying back, Jay C. Freeman's mistakes." [32] Rembert had not hired Mr. Freeman who had become by the mid 1930s "a dilemma" impairing the reputation of Wurlitzer.[33] Rembert was outraged, probably feeling his own reputation was also being demeaned.

In identifying a Stradivari forgery, a good ear was helpful, but not essential in recognizing the Stradivari sound, as when Rembert heard the red violin for the first time. The sound of the instrument enters only a little into determining authenticity. The sound of an instrument is greatly affected by condition, setup, the bow used, and whether or not a player is in touch with the instrument.

Oscilloscope sound patterns are not useful in confirming a Stradivari to be authentic. In the movie *The Red Violi,* oscilloscopes were used. That was misleading. Rembert did not use an oscilloscope.

All instruments that Antonio Stradivarius made bear a label written in Latin that reads, *"Antonius Stradivarius Cremonensis Faciebat Anno* [date]. " The label indicated the maker, the place of production, and the date. Rembert glued a number inside each Stradivarius violin. Rather than demeaning the value of a Stradivarius, the Wurlitzer label added value, because it indicated Rembert Wurlitzer authentication.

The wood used by Stradivarius was usually **maple infused** with minerals. Some claim this infusion is the reason replication of sound

---

[32]*Stradivari's Genius* by Toby Faber. Random House Paperback, New York. 2004.
    Page 194.
[33] https://www.gettyimages.ca/detail/news-photo/photo-shows-a-dilema-for-a-
    violin-expert-jay-c-freeman-news-photo/540340080.

has not been usually possible so far.[34] Others suggest it was how Antonio cut the "f" holes that creates the Stradivari sound.[35] Both aspects may contribute to a wonderful sound.

Stradivari violins now sell for many millions, far more than what Rembert paid. The highest price paid up to 2011 for a Stradivarius violin was the "*Lady Blunt*" Stradivarius of 1721, which sold for a record $16 million in 2011 to an anonymous buyer who loaned the violin to violinist Anne Akiko Meyers who is still alive. Earlier, in the 1890s, **W.E. Hill & Sons** had bought the violin from Lady Ann Blunt and sold it to an important collector, but not to the Wurlitzer Company or Rembert.

In 2019 Mr. Fulton's Foundation sold *La Pucelle* for **$22,000,000. Rembert had originally bought the fiddle in 1955 from Mr. Frank Otwell for $25,000.**[36] Stradivari instruments have on average increased greatly in value over time.

A rare viola made by Stradivari in 1719, The "MacDonald" Viola, owned at one time by The Rudolph Wurlitzer Company,[37] did not sell at the reserve price of $45 million set by Sotheby's in 2014. It was the first to be on the market in fifty years, according to Sotheby's auction house. It is also one of only two Stradivari violas still privately owned. The other is held in the Library of Congress in Washington, DC.

Stradivari instruments are indeed rare and immensely valuable, if not priceless. They are usually musical instruments of legend.

---

[34] https://www.asianscientist.com/2016/12/in-the-lab/stradivarius-violin-wood-mineral-preservative/.

[35] https://www.theregister.co.uk/2015/02/15/violin_acoustics_f_holes_mit/

[36] Private correspondence with Mr. David Fulton

[37] https://tarisio.com/cozio-archive/property/?ID=40262.

Provenances of Two Famous Stradivari Violins

Many Stradivari known to have been owned at one time by Rembert have interesting stories. We shall embark upon two of these stories, starting first with the Hammer Stradivari, *The Hammer,* and then with the Red Violin, *The Mendelssohn,* of 1720 and build my case further that this was the red violin Rembert discovered. In part, this ode to Rembert is a mystery story, because the complete provenance of *The Mendelssohn* is still very much unknown.

1. **ANTONIO STRADIVARI**
   A VIOLIN KNOWN AS *THE HAMMER*,
   CREMONA, 1707
   Labeled *Antonius Stradivarius Cremonensis/Faciebat Anno 1707*, length of back 14 inches (355 mm) with case
   (2) Tarisio #40643

   Provenance
   Christian Hammer
   Bernard Sinsheimer
   Raymond Pitcairn (whose Grand-niece Elizabeth owns
      The Mendelssohn)
   Albert Wallace
   Rembert Wurlitzer
   Laddie Junkunc
   Present Owner

Christie Auction house wrote, "The violin, referred to as *The Hammer*, derives its name from the first recorded owner, 19th-century Swedish collector, Christian Hammer. As court jeweler to the Swedish royal family, Christian Hammer was a collector with an insatiable appetite. During his lifetime, Hammer accumulated over 400,000 articles as varied as fine art, jewelry, books, and manuscripts. Though little is documented regarding his musical instrument collection, his existence was known to William E. Hill and Sons, who made mention of Hammer and this violin in *Antonio Stradivari, His Life and Work*, published in London in 1902.

In 1911, the violin was sold by the London firm of Hart & Son and brought to America by the violinist and teacher Bernard Sinsheimer. As well as being a celebrated soloist and chamber musician, Sinsheimer was a savvy collector who owned no fewer than five works by Stradivari during his career. The instrument later came into the possession of the collector, Raymond Pitcairn. The connoisseurship of Pitcairn is well documented. As a highly successful Philadelphia attorney, he owned two other Stradivari, as well as a 1737 Carlo Bergonzi and a Gasparo da Salo of 1570.

Both music and connoisseurship continue to be evident in the Pitcairn family. The great-niece of Raymond Pitcairn is violin virtuoso, Elizabeth Pitcairn, owner of the 1720 Stradivari known as *The Mendelssohn*. Purchased at Christie's London salesrooms in 1990, it was at the time the world auction record for a work by Stradivari.

In 1927, the *Hammer* passed to Albert H. Wallace through the New York dealer Emil Herrmann. A resident of Los Angeles, Wallace was also an important collector who possessed three other works by Stradivari as well as a Bergonzi and a Nicolo Amati. In 1945, the violin was sold by Rembert Wurlitzer to Chicago businessman Laddie Junkunc. There, the violin remained until 1992 when it came into possession of the present owner.

Purchased for philanthropic reasons, the *Hammer* was, until recently, on loan to violinist Kyoko Takezawa. A prolific recording artist and celebrated soloist, Ms. Takezawa used the *Hammer* Stradivari as her primary performance instrument."[38]

Many of the great Stradivari violins have engaging nicknames like *The Messiah, The Dolphin, The Virgin, The Lady Blunt, The Contessa, The Venus,* and *The Molitor* (owned by Bonaparte) that has added to the magical allure of these magnificent instruments. Sometimes, ownership ran in families, such as a Pitcairn who owned *The Hammer* and now violinist Elizabeth Pitcairn who owns *The Mendelssohn.* Often owners would loan Stradivari violins to famous violinists.

More than a few Stradivari have become legendary like *The Mendelssohn* and priceless or certainly irreplaceable to their owners. Rembert was indeed blessed to have owned so many of these superlative works of art.

In *The Rainaldi Quartet*, Paul Adam rhapsodizes about a Stradivari violin: "It's a work of art to rank alongside the *Mona Lisa, The Divine Comedy*, and the operas of Verdi. It's a masterpiece as great as anything Michelangelo produced, as profound as a Beethoven symphony, as sublime and universal as a Shakespeare tragedy." Indeed, Stradivari violins are great works of art.

2. ANTONIO STRADIVARI
A VIOLIN KNOWN AS *THE MENDELSSOHN* OR *RED MENDELSSOHN OF 1720*. CREMONA.

---

[38] https://www.christies.com/lotfinder/Lot/antonio-stradivari-a-violin-known-as-the-4705238-details.aspx.

Violinist Elizabeth Pitcairn is the owner of the 1720 Stradivari known as *The Mendelssohn.* Purchased at Christie's London salesrooms in 1990 for $1,700,000, it was at the time the world auction record for a work by Stradivari. The violin appeared to vanish after its creation for more than 100 years until I suggest it was discovered by Rembert in the 1920s in Berlin. Unfortunately, after writing her, Mme. Pitcairn could not be of help in developing the provenance of *The Mendelssohn* further.

My father's childhood languages were first German and secondly English. Rembert became fluent in German later. The two of them sometimes went to Germany in the 1920s for business, pleasure, or to visit family. There was the "Clarinet Wurlitzer," and in East Germany, many Wurlitzer relatives. Rudolph Henry had gone to violin school in Berlin, and Rembert followed with studies in Europe in the 1920s.

After East Germany opened up following reunification in 1990, I met Wurlitzers who had survived World War II. In Vienna, there were other Wurlitzers who lived on Wurlitzergasse (i.e., Wurlitzer Alley or Lane).[39] German connections were ongoing among American Wurlitzers, who often communicated with their German kin. My mother, whose first language was also German, did so routinely.

In 1960, Farny started in Hüllhorst a German branch of the Wurlitzer Company called "Deutsche Wurlitzer." That division became a reason for Farny, who became President in 1932, to go to Germany often until his death in 1972. The Gibson Guitar Corporation controls the Wurlitzer brand now.

---

[39] https://www.geschichtewiki.wien.gv.at/Wurlitzergasse.

Rembert, or another Wurlitzer, and my father would sometimes stop in Berlin. I have old, undated photos showing my father in Berlin sometime in the mid- or late-1920s before his father and my grandfather Howard died in 1928. My father left Wurlitzer in 1928 after his father, Howard, CEO of Wurlitzer, died.

Canadian filmmaker Francois Girard's imaginative speculations about *The Mendelssohn* and its 1990 Christie's auction became the narrative for the 1999 Academy Award-winning film, *The Red Violin*. Literally, none of the past history was known initially about *The Mendelssohn* after its resurrection in the 1920s.

In a program for a performance by Pitcairn with *The Mendelssohn*, Suzanne Marcus Fletcher wrote: "The historic violin was crafted in 1720 by Antonio Stradivari, who lovingly made his instruments in his small shop in Cremona, Italy centuries ago, and remains the most famous violin maker of all time. Not long after its creation, the instrument appeared to vanish; no one knows where or to whom the violin belonged for more than 200 years,[40] spawning any number of historians, writers, journalists, critics as well as Canadian filmmaker, Francois Girard, to speculate on the violin's mysterious history. Girard's imaginative speculations became the narrative for his beloved film, *The Red Violin*."

"Known as the *Red Stradivarius* and owned by legendary violinist Joseph Joachim, the 1720 *Red Mendelssohn* Stradivarius would eventually surface in 1920s Berlin. It had been purchased by an heir to the great composer, Felix Mendelssohn. In 1956, it was purchased by a New York industrialist (presumably referring to Rembert, as Tarisio records for #40316 possibly confirm) who kept the instrument in impeccable performance condition. Much of its original burnished red varnish remains on the violin today, and it is

---

[40] Two hundred years is incorrect. It was more like 100 years. Remember, please, the author did not write this blurb.

thought to be one of the best sounding and most beautiful of Stradivari's remaining violins. Then on Thanksgiving Day in 1990, the instrument's fate would once again be triggered when the industrialist (presumably referring to Rosenthal, Schube or Smith[41]) opted to put the Red Stradivarius on the auction block anonymously at Christie's of London. While some of the world's most powerful sought to win the coveted instrument, it landed in the hands of then sixteen-year-old American solo violinist, Elizabeth Pitcairn. Pitcairn would remain silent about owning the violin until her rapidly burgeoning solo career brought her into the public eye on international concert stages after nearly three decades of rigorous training by the world's most esteemed violin teachers."

"Pitcairn would come to view the violin as her life's most inspiring mentor and friend. Many have said that the violin has finally found its true soul mate in the gifted hands of the young violinist who is the first known solo artist to ever bring it to the great concert halls of the world, and who has made it her goal to share the violin's magical beauty of sound with people of all ages, professions, and cultures. Today, Pitcairn and the *Red Mendelssohn* Stradivarius violin continue to foster one of classical music's most compelling partnerships." – By Suzanne Marcus Fletcher

The story about *The Mendelssohn* continues with abated breath. Now the violin is listed in the auction house Tarisio's inventory in New York as item #40316.[42]

The provenance is interesting as cited by Tarisio and provocative as modified by me:

1. **Lilli von *Mendelssohn***

2. **Franz von *Mendelssohn***

---

[41] Goodkind, H.K. *Violin Iconography of Antonio Stradivari*. Page 734
[42] https://tarisio.com/cozio-archive/property/?ID=40316.

...Then, over a 100-year gap!

So where did the violin go? Who owned it after The Mendelssohns during that 100-year gap is largely speculation.

3. **Joseph Joachim**, the legendary violinist, dates unknown. Elizabeth Pitcairn lists Joachim as an owner.

...a 100-year gap

4. **Francesco Mendelssohn 1913**
   How did the Mendelssohn pass from Francesco? Read the play to find out.
5. **Rembert Wurlitzer? Early 1926?**

(*The Mendelssohn* or *The Red Violin* was found probably, in my opinion, sometime in the mid- or late-1920s in Berlin by Rembert before my father left Wurlitzer in 1928, since my father was with Rembert when he found a red violin. Nonetheless, it could have been in the 1930s. A very likely date is 1926 before Rembert, at the age of 22, was made head of Wurlitzer acquisitions, I suspect, in large part as a reward for having found a red Stradivarius violin. That violin was almost certainly *The Mendelssohn*, as it was later called.

Tarisio lists Rembert as having been the first owner of its Stradivarius violin #51374, one of the suspects as having been the real *Red Violin*.

Rembert would then have authenticated the red violin perhaps with his father, Rudolph Henry, who had gone to a violin school in Berlin. Then, I suggest, Rembert sold the violin at an unknown date to Hamma, later in 1926 or even less likely in the 1930s.

According to Tarisio, Rembert purchased *The Mendelssohn* violin (Tarisio #40316) from Hamma in 1956.

There could have been a later authentication as well if Rembert sold the violin to Luther Rosenthal and Son sometime after 1956. Tarisio records for red violin #51374 suggest that the red violin was sold in 1968 to Jacques Francais. Since Rembert died in 1963, it was probably Rembert's wife, Lee, who sold a red violin then. This somewhat speculative outline is expanded upon in the play *Rembert* that follows in Addenda III and IV.

6. **Hamma and Co.**, until 1956

Hamma records as to who sold them *The Mendelssohn* are unavailable. I suggest it was Rembert who found this legendary red violin, authenticated it with the help of his father Rudolph, a world-recognized rare violin expert, and then sold it to Walter Hamma in the mid or later 1920s, but before 1928 when my father left Wurlitzer shortly after his father Howard had died.

Publicity was unimportant. I suggest further Hamma would never have agreed to buy the violin originally around 1926 up to 1928 without Wurlitzer authentication from the world's two foremost experts, Rembert and Rudolph Henry, giving further circumstantial support that Rembert was involved with the violin at a very early point after its resurrection in the 1920s.

Unfortunately, there is no known written record today, to the best of my knowledge, of how Hamma obtained the violin to confirm my story. Tarisio affirms Rembert was the first owner of the red, unnamed Stradivarius #51374. If that violin is the same as *The Mendelssohn*, that would be confirmation Rembert found *The Mendelssohn*.

Admittedly, I have entered into speculation, but it is speculation based on common sense and knowledge of many particulars. The circumstantial evidence is very convincing Rembert owned a red Stradivarius violin of 1720. None of the four Stradivari violins of 1720 listed by Goodkind to have been handled by a Wurlitzer were recorded to have been red.

7. **Rembert Wurlitzer,** from 1956 until 1963 when he died. Tarisio records for The Mendelssohn Tarisio #40316 list Rembert after having become an owner in 1956. Then Tarisio #51374 shows Rembert sold a red violin, possibly *The Mendelssohn* to Jacques Francais in 1968. Since Rembert died in 1963, he could not have sold the violin in 1968. Presumably, his wife Lee sold the violin in 1968. Luthier Rosental and Son, Schube and Smith

8. *Lee* **Wurlitzer,** from 1963 to 1968. In 1968, Lee, the widow of Rembert, sold a red violin Tarisio #51374 to Jacques Francais, et al. I suspect, but have no proof, that the two Tarisio violins #40316 and #51374 are the same violin, *The Mendelssohn.*

9. **Jacques Francais** from 1968 to 1990? Luthier Rosental and Son, Schube and Smith are listed by Goodkind as owners. They may have been co-owners. Collating information from Tarisio and other records is not easy.

10. **Shube and then Smith,** ????. Goodkind lists these individuals as owners after Jacques Francais.

   Since Rembert passed away in 1963, Rembert could not
have had the violin personally up to 1990 as the Tarisio
provenances suggest for both violins #51374 and #40316. This
inconsistency is just another example of how provenances are
often incomplete.

   **11. Luther Rosenthal and Son, or Schube, and then
   Smith???,** from around 1968 until 1990. Goodkind
   does not give dates for owners.

   12. Elizabeth Pitcairn, from 1990 and Current Owner,
   Tarisio does not even list Pitcairn as a current owner.

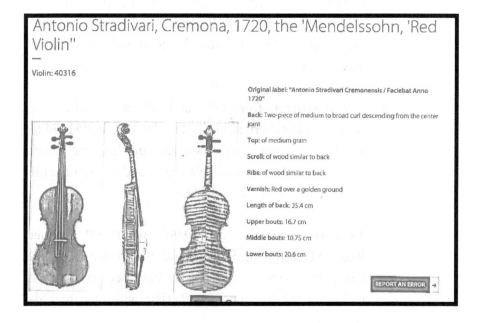

Antonio Stradivari, Cremona, 1720, the 'Mendelssohn, 'Red Violin"

Violin: 40316

Original label: "Antonio Stradivari Cremonensis / Faciebat Anno 1720"

Back: Two-piece of medium to broad curl descending from the center joint

Top: of medium grain

Scroll: of wood similar to back

Ribs: of wood similar to back

Varnish: Red over a golden ground

Length of back: 35.4 cm

Upper bouts: 16.7 cm

Middle bouts: 10.75 cm

Lower bouts: 20.6 cm

REPORT AN ERROR →

Tarisio Website

   This violin mystery story continues. How did Hamma and Co. get
a red Stradivari violin? Hamma records are unavailable. Neither
Elizabeth Pitcairn the current owner of The Mendelssohn, nor David

Fulton with his database of Wurlitzer records were of final help, nor could Marianne Wurlitzer, daughter of Rembert, help. All existent records available to me are confusing.

Did Rembert, after discovering a red violin in Berlin many years ago, sell the violin to Hamma in Stuttgart, Germany, as *The Mendelssohn* or just as another Stradivari violin after authenticating it? It is doubtful there are many other Stradivari violins that are as red as *The Mendelssohn* implicating this violin to be the red one Rembert found.

It is also doubtful that Hamma would have bought a Stradivarius violin without a Rembert and Rudolph Henry expert authentication, since Rudolph and Walter Hamma were long-time associates. Unfortunately, Tarisio does not have the original authentications that might have helped in confirming provenance further.

More than once, Rembert bought, sold, and then bought the same violin again as, for example, the Baron Knoop of 1715. The psychology that can be added to circumstantial arguments may be that it was easier for Rembert to buy in 1956 a violin he had already authenticated than one not previously authenticated by him. Walter Hamma may also have felt it was easier and more practical, or even that he was morally obligated, to sell *The Mendelssohn* in 1956 to Rembert, an eager buyer who had discovered and authenticated it. Rembert had the money and was well known for being fair. Stradivari are rarely bought or sold at bargain prices.

The fact that Rembert or Rudolph Henry, through Wurlitzer, and Rembert on his own through the Rembert Wurlitzer Company, handled, authenticated, held on consignment, and/or sold 135 Stradivari violins is awesome. There is no other history known to me of ownership coming close to Rembert's record ever for owning or controlling through consignments Stradivari instruments, although admittedly, Rembert did not obviously own or control all these

Stradivari violins at the same time. Many violins were on consignment. This fact that Rembert owned, handled or sold unequivocally an extraordinary number of Stradivari violins qualifies calling Rembert "The Stradivarius Wurlitzer." If W.H. Hill, Hamma, or any other dealer can be shown to have handled more violins I would defer to them and call that dealer, "The Stradivarius Dealer."

The evidence that Rembert discovered *The Mendelssohn* in the 1920s is very convincing. But if proof surfaces otherwise that *The Mendelssohn* was not discovered by Rembert sometime in the 1920s or even in the 1930s, then I would withdraw my suggested change in provenance, although insisting that the story of a red violin found by Rembert as related to me by my father was true and not hearsay. Then my question would be, what red Stradivari violin was it that Rembert discovered in the 1920s?

There is another suspect in mind, the "*Unnamed*" Stradivarius (Tarisio #51374), whose provenance begins with Rembert. Is it not a curious coincidence that *The Unnamed* and *The Mendelssohn* were made in 1720? It would be indeed interesting if Tarisio #51374 and Tarisio #40316 were the same violin. But based on color and the circumstantial evidence presented, I feel there is no more likely suspect than *The Mendelssohn*. That is my conclusion to this mystery story and ode to Rembert.

I, a music-loving Wurlitzer, regret I do not own a Stradivarius violin and, in particular, *The Mendelssohn*, also known to me presumptuously as *The Red Wurlitzer Mendelssohn*. I know I could not afford to buy it anyway, even if it is ever on the market again.

Fred Wurlitzer, M.D., F.A.C.S., M.B.A.
Grandson of Howard Eugene Wurlitzer
First Cousin once removed of Rembert Wurlitzer

Appendix I

List of 135[43] Stradivari Violins Owned or Sold by a Wurlitzer

The first two violins marked with an asterisk (*) have had their provenances revised. Caveats exist, so bear with me please.

Often Goodkind records did not match Tarisio records. Many times, Tarisio did not give credit to Goodkind listing Wurlitzer as an owner or seller. Many times also, Goodkind descriptions of a violin were not the same as those used by Tarisio, and finally, many times, references listed by Goodkind were not in the less-extensive Tarisio database.

More credence was given to Goodkind than to Tarisio because of the obvious thoroughness and scholarship of Goodkind. Moreover, Goodkind was a personal friend of Rembert, visiting him often. Goodkind had greater access to Rembert than Tarisio auction house.

Although Tarisio had far fewer references to Stradivari violins than Goodkind, I believe a fairly exhaustive list was created by collating my two primary sources, Tarisio and Goodkind, for Stradivari violins handled or sold by a Wurlitzer. That is not to say I am representing the list is conclusive. Repeated efforts were taken to avoid duplications and to be accurate.

When both Tarisio and Goodkind reported a Stradivari violin to have been owned by a Wurlitzer, there should be little doubt in the authenticity of that mutual representation. It remains odd, though, that there should be so many discrepancies. Countless times, Goodkind would list Wurlitzer as an owner or seller, while Tarisio would not confirm this representation, and vice versa.

---

[43] 136 Stradivari violins are listed, but two violins are the same as explained shortly in the Apology, making the number 135. Actually, Marianne Wurlitzer sold a Stradivarius that is not listed, but is referenced in the play *Rembert* that follows in Addenda III and IV.

This listing of Stradivari violins handled or sold by a Wurlitzer has been very time-consuming. One of the barriers to entry of undertaking this task was the expense of the Goodkind book running up to a thousand dollars or more. I was fortunate to obtain an autographed Goodkind book of his *Violin Iconography of Antonio Stradivari*. Without doubt, the Goodkind book has the most exhaustive list of Stradivari violins of any book published on the subject.

No one, to the best of my knowledge, has ever previously developed such a collated list of Stradivari violins handled, authenticated, or sold by a Wurlitzer, primarily Rembert Wurlitzer.

At the end of the play that follows, I present a provenance of *The Mendelssohn* developed by Mr. David Fulton of Seattle. His provenance does not include any owners between 1913, when Francesco Mendelssohn owned *The Mendelssohn*, and 1990 when Elizabeth Pitcairn came into possession of *The Mendelssohn*. In the List that follows I do not give the provenance of *The Mendelssohn* prior to Rembert's first ownership around 1926.

Abbreviations

WNLT = Wurlitzer Not Listed by Tarisio; WNLG = Wurlitzer Not
Listed by
Goodkind
(S) = Sold by Wurlitzer, not necessarily owned; Goodkind/T = Listed by
both Goodkind and Tarisio

Year	Sobriquet	Provenance	Notes or Tarisio #
		Antionio Stradivari Violins	
1720	*The Mendelssohn**	Lilli von Mendelssohn	40316
		Franz von Mendelssohn	
		Over a 100-year gap	
		Rembert Wurlitzer ??	This violin was found, perhaps, by Rembert. Hamma records are unavailable. I suggest Rembert sold it to Hamma since Rembert passed away in 1963
		Until 1956 Hamma & Co.	
		From 1956 Rembert W.	
		Until 1990 Luther Rosenthal and son	
		From 1990 Current owner	

Year	Sobriquet	Provenance	Notes or Tarisio #
1709	*La Pucelle**	Freddie Herman	40212
		Until 1851 Jean-Baptiste Vuillaume	
		in 1870 Glandaz	
		In 1878 Sold by Hotel Drouot	
		From 1878 Unknown	
		In 1903 Sold by Caressa & Francais	
		1903-1904 W.E. Hill & Sons	
		From 1904 Richard C. Baker	
		Until 1942 W.E. Hill & Sons	
		1942-1946 Robert Augustus Bower	
		From 1946 Frank Otwell	

	Not listed on Tarisio	**1953 Rembert Wurlitzer?**	Loaned to La Salle Sept. 20, 1953 on consignment. Bought on 5/11/1955
		1956 Anna E. Clark	
		Huguette M. Clark	
		From 2001 David L. Fulton. Fulton Foundation sold it 2019 for $22 million	
1679	*The Hellier*	Rembert Wurlitzer	40237
1681	*Chanot-Chardon*	Goodkind/T	41488
1681	*Reynier*	Goodkind/T Rudolph	40675
1682	*Hill, Banat*	Rembert Wurlitzer	41257
1683	*Martinelli, Gingold*	Rudolph Wurlitzer	40473
1683	*Madame Bastard*	Wurlitzer by Goodkind	WNLT
1684	*Soames*	Goodkind/T Rudolph	40742
1685	*MacKenzie, Castelbarco*	Rembert Wurlitzer	40756
1685	*Becker; Florentiner*	Goodkind/T Rudolph	40750
1685	*Marquis*	Goodkind/T Rudolph	40470
1687	*Marie Law*	Wurlitzer by Goodkind	41431

1688	*Derenberg*	Rembert Wurlitzer	40760
1690	*The Theodor*	Rembert Wurlitzer	41446
1690	*Stephens*	Goodkind/T Rudolph	40726
1693	*Harrison*	Rembert Wurlitzer	40039
1694	*Irish, Burgundy, St. Sebastian*	Rembert Wurlitzer	40783
1695	*Goetz; Hawaiian*	Goodkind/T Rudolph	40785
1696	*Vornbaum, Weinberger*	Wurlitzer by Goodkind	WNLT
1697	*Montbel*	Rembert Wurlitzer	41321
1697	*Uchtomsky*	Goodkind/T Rudolph	41263
1698	*Lark*	Goodkind/T Rudolph	41266
1698	*Schumann*	Goodkind/T Rudolph	40472
1698	*Greiner*	Goodkind/T Rudolph	WNLT
1698	*Joachim;Kortschalk*	Goodkind/T Rudolph	40474
1699	*Contesssa, de Polignac*	Rembert Wurlitzer	40125
1699	*La Font #1*	Goodkind/T Rudolph	40274
1700	*Jupiter*	Rudolph Wurlitzer	41306
1700	*Taft; van Donop; Ward*	Wurlitzer by Goodkind	40116
1701	*Circle*	Wurlitzer by Goodkind	41312
1701	*Johnson, Dushkin, Sandler*	Goodkind/T Rudolph	40079

1702	*King Maximilian Joseph*	Rembert Wurlitzer	40080
1703	*Alsager*	Goodkind/T Rudolph	41318
1703	*Montbel*	Goodkind/T Rudolph	41321
1703	*de Rougement #1*	Wurlitzer by Goodkind	40478
1703	*de Rougement #2, Ford*	Goodkind/T Rudolph	40257
1704	*Betts*	Goodkind/T Rudolph	40118
1704	*Viotti*	Wurlitzer by Goodkind	41327
1705	*Baron von der Leyen*	Rembert Wurlitzer	31299
1707	*The Hammer*	Rembert Wurlitzer	40643
1707	*Dragonetti; Rivaz*	Wurlitzer by Goodkind	40057
1708	*The Ruby*	Rembert Wurlitzer	40084
1708	*Balakovic, Soll, Strauss*	Wurlitzer by Goodkind	41156
1708	*Dancla*	Wurlitzer by Goodkind	43076
1708	*Huggins*	Goodkind/T Rudolph	40053
1709	*Ernst*	Goodkind/T Rudolph	40287
1709	*Siberian; The Jack*	Goodkind/T Rudolph	41350
1710	*MacKenzie, Castelbarco*	Rembert Wurlitzer	40756
1710	*Berger, Dancla*	Goodkind/T Rudolph	43077
1711	*Earl of Plymouth, Kreisler*	Rembert Wurlitzer	44058

1712	*Darnley, Eldina Bligh*	Rudolph Wurlitzer	41371
1712	*Hrimali, Press*	Rembert Wurlitzer	41378
1712	*Viotti*	Wurlitzer by Goodkind	40288
1713	*Gaglione; Hill*	Wurlitzer by Goodkind	WNLT
1713	*Soncy; Kubelik*	Wurlitzer by Goodkind	40491
1713	*Rodewald*	Wurlitzer by Goodkind	WNLT
1713	*Pingrille*	Wurlitzer by Goodkind	40492
1713	*Havemeyer*	Wurlitzer by Goodkind	WNLT
1714	*Kneisel, Grun*	Rembert Wurlitzer	23286
1714	*Dolphin or Delfino*	Rembert Wurlitzer	29483
1714	*Joachim Ma*	Rembert Wurlitzer	40496
1714	*Adam*	Wurlitzer by Goodkind	41383
1715	*Lipinski*	Rembert Wurlitzer	40497
1715	*Baron Knoop, Bevan*	Rembert Wurlitzer	41471
1715	*The Lipinski*	Rembert Wurlitzer	40497
1715	*Hochstein*	Wurlitzer by Goodkind	41390
1715	*Titian*	Goodkind/T Rudolph	41393
1716	*Otto Booth, Cho-Ming Sin*	Rembert Wurlitzer	40057
1716	*Cessole*	Rembert Wurlitzer	41398

1716	*The Serdet*	Rembert Wurlitzer	41967
1717	*The Reiffenberg*	Rembert Wurlitzer	41538
1717	*Duchess*	Wurlitzer by Goodkind	WNLT
1717	*Fite; Windsor*	Wurlitzer by Goodkind	40439
1717	*Gariel*	Wurlitzer by Goodkind	41424
1717	*Matthews*	Wurlitzer by Goodkind	WNLT
1717	*Mercadente*	Wurlitzer by Goodkind	WNLT
1717	*Piatti*	Goodkind/T Rudolph	40503
1717	*Toenniges*	Wurlitzer by Goodkind	WNLT
1718	*Mylnarski*	Wurlitzer by Goodkind	41478
1718	*Tyrell; Speyer*	Wurlitzer by Goodkind	40508
1718	*Wilmotte*	Goodkind/T Rudolph	43091
1719	*Wickett; Wurlitzer*	Wurlitzer by Goodkind	WNLT
1720	*Bavarian*	Rembert Wurlitzer	41488
1720	*Unamed*	Rembert Wurlitzer	51374
1720	*L'Eveque*	Goodkind/T Rudolph	40517
1720	*Madrileno*	Goodkind/T Rudolph	43093
1720	*Woolhouse*	Wurlitzer by Goodkind	41489
1721	*The Mercadent*	Rembert Wurlitzer	43086

1721	*Archinto*	Goodkind/T Rudolph	41500
1721	*Vidoudez, Maazel, Artol*	Wurlitzer by Goodkind	40210
1722	*Cadiz; Cannon; Wilmotte*	Wurlitzer by Goodkind	40527
1722	*de Chapenay*	Wurlitzer by Goodkind	40291
1722	*Earl of Westmorland*	Goodkind/T Rudolph	40523
1722	*Elman*	Wurlitzer by Goodkind	41503
1723	*Kiesewetter*	Rembert Wurlitzer	40085
1723	*Joachim, Elman*	Goodkind/T Rudolph	41503
1723	*McCormack; Edler*	Goodkind/T Rudolph	41514
1725	*The Koeber*	Rembert Wurlitzer	43099
1725	*Bott; Cambridge*	Goodkind/T Rudolph	40528
1725	*Lubbock*	Goodkind/T Rudolph	41520
1725	*Wilhelm*	Wurlitzer by Goodkind	40060
1727	*Kreutzer*	Goodkind/T Rudolph	40535
1727	*The Venus*	Rembert Wurlitzer	41530
1727	*DuPont*	Wurlitzer by Goodkind	41154
1727	*Smith; Wendling; Barrett*	Wurlitzer by Goodkind	41546
1727	*Venus; Cho-Ming Sin*	Wurlitzer by Goodkind	WNLT

1728	*Villefranche*	Wurlitzer by Goodkind	WNLT
1729	*Benny; Artot Alard*	Wurlitzer by Goodkind	43102
1729	*Libon; Stuart; Dickinson*	Wurlitzer by Goodkind	41544
1730	*Johnson; Royal Spanish*	Wurlitzer by Goodkind	49637
1731	*Garcin*	Wurlitzer by Goodkind	41500
1731	*Romanoff; Maurin*	Wurlitzer by Goodkind	40249
1732	*Alcontara*	Goodkind/T Rudolph	41405
1732	*Taylor*	Goodkind/T Rudolph	40541
1733	*des Rossiers*	Goodkind/T Rudolph	40677
1734	*Lam, Scotland*	Rembert Wurlitzer	41367
1734	*Ames*	Wurlitzer by Goodkind	40545
1734	*Amherst*	Goodkind/T Rudolph	40544
1734	*Scotland University*	Wurlitzer by Goodkind	41567
1735	*Nestor, Leveque, Rode*	Rembert Wurlitzer	40533
1735	*Lamoureux*	Goodkind/T Rudolph	40546
1736	*Doria, Armingaud*	Rembert Wurlitzer	43108
1737	*Swan Song*	Rudolph Wurlitzer	40540
1737	*Lord Norton*	Rembert Wurlitzer	41574
1737	*d'Armaille*	Wurlitzer by Goodkind	41575

1737	*Norton*	Wurlitzer by Goodkind	41574
1743	*Baron Knoop*	Rembert Wurlitzer	41411

Nine Sons of Stradivari Violins Owned by Rembert				
Year	Maker (Stradivari)	Sobriquet	Source	Tarisio #
1734	Francesco	*TC Peterson*	Wurlitzer by Goodkind	45521
1736	Omobono	*?*	Rembert Wurlitzer	43108
1738	Omobono	*Tanocky Kazarian*	Wurlitzer by Goodkind	41595
1740	Omobono	*Zarontin*	Wurlitzer by Goodkind	None
1740	Omobono	*Weiner; Paul*	Wurlitzer by Goodkind	43114
1740	Omobono	*Frecke*	Wurlitzer by Goodkind	None
1740	Omobono	*Gulina*	Wurlitzer by Goodkind	None
1740	Omobono	*Leveque*	Wurlitzer by Goodkind	None
1742	Francesco	*Le Besque*	Rembert Wurlitzer	42845

Appendix II

Resources

1. *Stradivari* by Stewart Pollens. Cambridge University Press 2010. This is an exhaustively researched book with details about Stradivari manufacturing that may overwhelm readers because of the thoroughness. Beautifully colored photos of some Stradivari are included. Provenances are very sketchy.

2. "*Violin Iconography of Antonio Stradivari. 1644-1737.* Treatises on the Life and Work of the "Patriarch" of Violinmakers. Inventory of 700 Known or Recorded Stradivari String Instruments." Index of 3,500 Names of Past or Present Stradivari Owners. Photographs of 400 Stradivari instruments with 1,500 Views. 1972. Cloth in slipcase. Inscribed by Herbert K. Goodkind with TLS. Paperback – 1972. This is a very pricey book that costs usually $600 U.S. or more. Its index is marvelous and far more extensive than the Tarisio records.

3. *The Rainaldi Quartet*: Gianni & Gustafest #1 (Giannia & Gustafeste) by Paul Adam July 1, 2007.

4. *Stradivari's Genius: Five Violins, One Cello* by Tony Faber

5. *Antonio Stradivari – the Celebrated Violin Maker* by Francois-Joseph Fétis. 2013 Dover Publications.

6. *The Violin: A Social History of the World's Most Versatile Instrument* by David Schoenbaum. Hardcover

7. *Violins of Hope:* Violins of the Holocaust--Instruments of Hope and Liberation in Mankind's Darkest... by James A. Grymes Paperback

8. *The Violin Maker:* Finding a Centuries-Old Tradition in a Brooklyn Workshop, Marchese, John

9. *Known Violin Makers* 7th Edition by John H. Fairfield, self-published. This book is fascinating to me because of citations of early Wurlitzer music instrument makers.

10. *A Thousand Mornings of Music* by Arnold Gingrich

11. Tariso auction house inventories at tarisio.com

12. Wikipedia List of Stradavari musical instruments at https://en.wikipedia.org/wiki/List_of_Stradivarius_instruments

13. William Griess, Grandson of Rudolph Henry Wurlitzer. Proofreader and information contributor.

14. *The Wurlitzer Family Grave Sites* by Terry Hathaway, an expert on automated music instruments. Published by Mechanicalmusicpress.

15. Friedericke Philipson of the Musikinstrumenten-Museum in Markneukirchen

16. *The Lady of the Casa, The Biography of Helene V.B. Wurlitzer* by John Scolie. The Rydal Press, 1959.

17. *Wurlitzer Family History* by Lloyd Graham 1955

18. *Antonio Stradivari – His Life and Work (1644 – 1737)* by W. Hill, Arthur Hill and Alfred Hill. 1965 by Dover Publications.

19. *Wurlitzer Family History* by Lloyd Graham May 1955 Published by Always Junkin'

20. *Wurlitzer of Cincinnati – The Name that Means Music to Millions* by Mark Palkovic. 2015 Published by the History Press.

21. Private correspondence with Marianne Wurlitzer, daughter of Rembert Wurlitzer

22. *The Violin Maker – Finding a Centuries-Old Tradition In A Brooklyn Workshop* by John Marchese. HarperCollings Publishers 2007

23. Private correspondence with Mr. David Fulton of Seattle in June 2020.

24. *Adventures of a Cello* by Carlos Prieto. University of Texas Press. October 1, 2006

25. *Stradivari, his Life and Work* by Hill 1902

Addendum I

An Apology with a Eureka Moment

Comparison of *Unnamed* (Tarisio #51374)
and *The Mendelssohn* (Tarisio #40316)

Are these Two Different Violins Actually the Same Violin?
The answer is certainly **YES! Eureka!**

Marianne, the daughter of Rembert, wrote to me on 4/2/2020 that she did not recall that her father had handled (or owned or held on consignment) *The Mendelssohn*. Her assertion seemed to be an existential threat to my book, *The Real Red Violin: A True Story About Rembert, the "Stradivarius Wurlitzer."* I became depressed.

Written records suggest she was not mistaken. Tarisio records for *The Mendelssohn* (Tarisio #40316) clearly show Rembert had bought *The Mendelssohn* from Herr Hamma in 1956. Tarisio records for the unnamed red Stradivarius #51374 state Rembert had been the first owner. Could the two Tarisio violins be the same violin? How could I explain the mystery of how Marianne could not recall *The Mendelssohn* being in inventory.

Goodkind[44] shows a Wurlitzer was involved with four Stradivari: *The Bishop, The Bavarian, The Madrileno*, and *The Woolhouse*. None of these violins have the same back patterns as shown in the Goodkind book. None of them have a back pattern similar to that of *The Mendelssohn*.

---

[44] Goodkind, H.K. *Violin Iconography of Antonio Stradivari*. Page 734

The Mendelssohn is not listed by Goodkind as having been in a Wurlitzer inventory. How could this be? Although I knew the Goodkind records were incomplete, *The Mendelssohn* was certainly in one Wurlitzer inventory or another at one time – or if not in an inventory, it, or an unaccounted red violin, had been in Rembert's possession. I had the advantage over others knowing what my father had told me – Rembert had found an unnamed red violin in Berlin. This was a fact to me. It was not conjecture. I really didn't care what records showed or didn't show.

According to Elizabeth Pitcairn,[45] "An industrialist bought '*The Red Mendelssohn*' in 1956 and owned it until it sold at an auction in 1990 for $1.7 million." That statement is inaccurate. The industrialist who bought the red violin in 1956 was Rembert, as cited by Tarisio for their violin #40316 known as *The Mendelssohn*. But Rembert did not sell the red violin in 1990, because he had died many years earlier in 1963.

According to Tarisio, Rembert sold Tarisio violin #51374, an unnamed Stradivarius of 1720 listing Rembert as the first owner, to Jacques Francais in 1968. The industrialist who sold the violin in 1990 was a different industrialist, either Rosenthal and Son, Schube, or Smith. Rembert could not have sold the red violin in 1968 or 1990, because he died in 1963. How could there be such confusion?

The answer came to me in part one sleepless morning. I had always considered two primary suspects for the *Red Stradivarius*, one I called *The Unnamed* (Tarisio #51374), and the second suspect was *The Mendelssohn* (Tarisio #40316). I had wondered often, and that night I wondered strongly in my sleep if they were the same violin. When I awoke, I asked myself, "What about the backs?" Sometimes,

---

[45] https://pamplinmedia.com/pt/11-features/240821-107379-acclaimed-violinist-pitcairn-
plays-with-famed-red-piece

we can look at information time after time, and then suddenly we collate information with insight.

It is now clear that both violins are the same violin. If Rembert had the violin in his inventory briefly, it was under a different name, an unnamed name other than *The Mendelssohn*. In my dream, he had not put his red violin in any inventory.

The backs of both violins are the same. Coincidentally, both violins (Tarisio #51374 and 40316) were made in 1720, giving further credence they are the same violin. Measurements for both violins were unavailable.

Nonetheless, Tarisio definitely confirms Rembert had owned both violins, Tarisio #51374 and #40316. Was it possible the two violins were the same? The answer after study was definitely yes.

Then the history of *The Mendelssohn* could be amplified by combining the two records. Goodkind's and Rembert's records were obviously incomplete. Rembert had owned the *The Mendelssohn* when he did not know for sure it was *The Mendelssohn*. It would have been listed briefly, possibly in an original Wurlitzer Music Company inventory, as simply an unnamed Stradivarius of 1720.

But Rembert may not have put his red violin in even the Wurlitzer inventory if he found it and bought it before he worked for Wurlitzer. It was his violin, not Wurlitzer's. It would have been inappropriate to list it in Wurlitzer inventory. If he sold it for more than what he paid for it, he would have kept the profits.

This scenario suggested strongly Rembert found his red violin in 1926 or the year before. One of the reasons I felt he had been hired to be head of Wurlitzer acquisitions in 1926 was based upon his proven expertise in finding this red Stradivarius.

Later in 1956, when Rembert bought it from Hamma, he did know the provenance better, but he did not list it in his inventory presumably for personal reasons. In the play that follows, I speculate what those reasons may have been. Basically, he felt the red violin was a "keeper" not to be placed in an inventory of violins awaiting sale.

The violin I call *The Unnamed of 1720* (Tarisio #51374)

***The Mendelssohn* of 1720 (Tarisio #40316)**

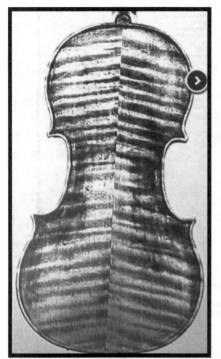

Close-up of *The Unnamed* back　　　**Close-up of *The Mendelssohn* back**

These photos were not taken at the same distance by me of the Tarisio originals, so one cannot judge apparent sizes. Clearly, the patterns are identical. Both violins are the same.

Tarisio gives the dimensions for *The Mendelssohn*, but not for *The Unnamed*, so, I am unable to compare dimensions. Nonetheless, the patterns of stripes are so similar that I feel comfortable asserting the two violins are one.

This is an astounding coincidence that strongly suggests Rembert obscured, hid, or did not acknowledge ownership of *The Mendelssohn* in his inventory leading Goodkind, Tarisio, and his daughter Marianne to assert Rembert had not owned *The Mendelssohn*. Rembert may have left *The Mendelssohn* unnamed originally as the provenance for

Tarisio #51374 strongly suggests, or he simply did not enter it into any inventory.

This may not have been purposeful obscuration. It may be that when Rembert bought *The Unnamed* (a.k.a. *The Mendelssohn*) in 1956, he did not know it was *The Mendelssohn*. There is no doubt from Tarisio records that Rembert bought *The Mendelssohn*. The Tarisio history of the unnamed Stradivarius #51374 cites Rembert as the first owner, giving strong credence to the argument that the *Real Red Violin* Rembert found was actually *The Mendelssohn*.

Both Goodkind and Tarisio did not recognize this error, and that led to great difficulty in identifying the *Real Red Violin*. Identifying the *Real Red Violin* has not been an easy task. I am now satisfied that the red violin my father told me Rembert discovered was indeed *The Mendelssohn.*

The account in the book, *The Real Red Violin,* I wrote initially as partially a mystery is in large part now no longer a mystery story. What fully happened around the time of Rembert's discovery is in part speculation, so I decided to make it into a play relating what I think happened.

With this discovery, so as to avoid double accounting, a Wurlitzer (either Rembert and/or Rudolph through The Wurlitzer Company), owned, handled, or sold at least 135 Stradivari violins. In the first edition of my book, *The Real Red Violin,* I had listed 136. Actually, the 136 number would be correct if one added the *Maia Bang* Stradivarius that Marianne Wurlitzer later found and sold. The *Maia Bang* is not listed in the inventories.

I was left with two options, the first being to rewrite the book, and the second being to submit "An Apology" as an addendum. I chose to apologize. That was simpler than making extensive revisions to the first book.

Along the way of my journey writing a detective story about Rembert, I felt that my story could not be finished without completing a play. Poetic license was taken in writing a play based on real and circumstantial evidence. It became my first attempt at writing a play, in this case based upon a romance story of Rembert in love with a violin.

In the play, I relate that Rembert found the red violin in 1926. It could not have been later because Raimund who was present with Rembert retired later in 1928. W.H. Hill heard about Rembert's find and made him a job offer – or W.H. Hill made a job offer because of Rembert's expertise when he worked with Hill. I could not confirm the exact date of the W.H. Hill job offer to Rembert.

Rembert's success in finding a red Stradivarius confirmed to the Wurlitzer Board that Rembert should be made head of acquisitions for Wurlitzer. That appointment in 1926 was made also to prevent W.H. Hill from hiring Rembert. It was a reward, too, for having proven his competence by finding a red Stradivarius.

In the play, facts fit together very well with speeulation. The actual year Rembert found the red violin could have been 1925 as well as 1926, but surely before Howard died and my father left Wurlitzer in 1928.

Fred Wurlitzer
June 4, 2020

Addendum II

INTERMEZZO

The Real Red Violin: A True Story About Rembert, the "Stradivarius Wurlitzer," was written as a history of Rembert Wurlitzer, a young man who discovered a red Stradivarius, and who, over time, became obsessed with rare violins. There is very little speculation in this book.

Addendum I, "An Apology," which precedes this, was added reflecting a problem with mistaken identity.

What follows is a play simply called *Rembert* that outlines what I think really happened using circumstantial and real evidence presented in the book. It is a play that follows Rembert from the time he went to Princeton to his death caused by a heart attack at age 59.

Although based mostly on facts, the play *Rembert* is still very much a speculative journey following Rembert's life through imagined conversations.

Poetic license was taken as I projected through dialogue and timelines what really happened in my opinion. I suggest that in many ways the play is more realistic and true to life than the recorded history, which is clouded by innumerable inconsistencies in recorded inventories by Rembert, Goodkind and others of Stradivari violins.

It is my hope that the play, *Rembert,* will be produced someday. It is the first play I've ever written.

Because of the quarantine imposed by COVID-19, I became tired of television and reading and found time to write. Without a COVID-19 quarantine, I doubt I would have written the book and the play. Then I would have been left with an unease that my father's story about Rembert finding a red violin had never been developed into a reality, rather than a fantasy play.

Writing the play saved me from going stir-crazy.

Fred Wurlitzer April 10, 2020

Prologue

(Part fiction, Part truth)

Francesco Mendelssohn was a confirmed alcoholic. But he was also a brave and forgetful alcoholic. Rembert knew him well. Francesco has become a very entertaining character in the play.

Francesco's father was a nephew of composer Felix Mendelssohn. In a bizarre turn of fate, Francesco purchased *The Mendelssohn*, a violin his great uncle Felix had owned from Wilhelm Hermann Hammig in 1913. Sometime after 1913, I speculate Francesco lost *The Mendelssohn* in a drunken stupor.

One-time in the late 1930's, Francesco smuggled his famous Stradivarius *Piatti cello* across the border from Germany into Switzerland on his bicycle. From Switzerland he went to New York where he met Rembert.[46]

Often Francesco would leave *the Piatti* in bars as ways of settling tabs. He may have told Rembert later that he didn't smuggle The *Mendelssohn*, because in our play the author speculates Francesco had lost that violin years earlier. After all, the *Mendelssohn* was more valuable in the late 1930's than the *Piatti Cello*, so surely he would have smuggled the Mendelssohn rather than the Piatti. He had no room on his bicycle for two instruments. It is a fact Francesco smuggled the *Piatti*. Why not the *Mendelssohn*? What happened to *The Mendelssohn* after 1913 when records show Francesco had owned it?

It is well known that one night after a concert in New York around 1950, Francesco tried to enter his home on East 62nd St. He became

---

[46] Adventures of a Cello by Carlos Prieto. University of Texas Press. 2006

frustrated. He was unable to open his front door. Awakening to the fact despite being in an alcoholic stupor that he was at the wrong house, he left his cello on the footpath as he staggered off to his own home.

The next morning his housekeeper awoke him and asked if a cello she has found on the street was his. "I found it in the street, just as the garbage truck was about to pick it up," she said. Francesco may not have even thanked her.[47]

It is the author's fantasy that Francesco didn't dare tell anyone, well maybe his wife, about a similar episode in 1913. After a concert he became alarmingly inebriated. Foolishly, he left the *Mendelssohn* on the street before his home in Germany. A garbage collector that time picked up the violin and later sold it to a gypsy.

Francesco apparently believed in leaving Stradivari instruments on streets for garbage collectors or in bars to assure later payments. Maybe, he left the violin on the Berlin street to assure the garbage collectors he would pay them. In any event, he didn't complain to authorities in Germany then, because he was Jewish. Maybe, he didn't complain because he had been utterly besotted and stupid.

Francesco also enjoyed pawning Stradivari instruments in bars to pay for alcohol and buy them back later. I find that attribute entertaining. It is even partially understandable since Strads weren't as monetarily valuable back then as they are today.

Freddie Beare, whose father had worked with Wurlitzer, recalls Rembert insisted when Francesco was planning a trip that he not take the Piatti Cello with him.[48] Rembert offered instead an instrument he

---

[47] https://www.irishtimes.com/culture/memoirs-of-a-stradivarius-1.932980
[48] This story was related to me by Mr. David Fulton.

had made in Mirecourt as a youth. Francesco accepted. Then in another drunken stupor, I like to think, while smoking, Francesco set unintentionally the dwelling he was in on fire. Rembert's instrument burned. The Piatti was saved, thanks to Rembert. Humanity was spared the loss of another Stradivarius.[49]

Francesco was clearly a threat to precious musical instruments. He was by all accounts entertaining but dangerous when musical instruments were in his possession. *The Piatti* was red and was known as the "*red cello.*" So is *The Red Mendelssohn.* Maybe, Francesco just didn't like to see red. Maybe, he became red in the face when he saw red. Maybe, unconscioiusly he always wanted to make red disappear when he saw it.

It may be also that no concert cellists ever wanted to loan Francesco an instrument, although he was an excellent cellist. "Buyer beware" became "player beware" in his presence.

In a further bizarre twist of fate, the author speculates that very same gypsy, who bought *The Mendelssohn* from a Berlin trash collector, played the Chaconne for Rembert and Raimund in an outdoor Berlin café in 1926. In appreciation, after of course another round of drinks, Francesco later called Rembert, "The Resurrector of the *Mendelssohn.*" Then the instrument was in Rembert's reliable hands, and especially so when many years later it was sold to Mr. Pitcairn who gave it to his daughter Elizabeth.

Rembert never entered the violin into any inventory. When he found it in 1926, he was not working for Wurlitzer. Later he refused to enter it into his own inventory, because it was "a keeper." Items entered

---

[49] Mr. David Fulton in editing my work asked that I insert this story about Francesco.

into inventory were meant to be sold, but not his beloved *Mendelssohn.*

There is little doubt Rembert was the first owner of an unnamed red violin, probably the Stradivarius (Tarisio #51374). According to Tarisio he also bought *The Mendelssohn* (Tarisio #40316) from Hamma in 1956. Ironically, both Tarisio violins are the same violin, *The Mendelssohn*. The later years of provenance for the *Mendelssohn* can be developed by collating the two Tarisio histories. Rembert's stock cards give little help.

Inventories and provenances are often disturbingly incomplete.

From the Irish times referenced above.

Memoirs of a Stradivarius Piatti Cello

"Tue, Jan 29, 2008

"From Italy to New York, Spain to Carlow, the biography of the Piatti cello made by Stradivari is a lively tale unearthed by its present owner, Mexican cellist Carlos Prieto, writes **Arminta Wallace**

Some stories you couldn't make up. If, for example, you were going to concoct the history of an eminent and hugely valuable Stradivarius, you probably wouldn't mix in a 19th-century Irish sherry merchant by the name of Don Alonso Dowell, an opera company in 18th-century Spain, a Carlow clergyman and an alcoholic New York socialite who was a relative of the composer Felix Mendelssohn. These, however, are just a few incidents from the real-life story of the 288-year-old instrument known as the Piatti cello - as related by its owner, the celebrated Mexican cellist Carlos Prieto, in his book *The Adventures of a Cello.*

"Prieto will talk about the book - and his reasons for writing it - at the John Field Room in the National Concert Hall next Monday at 8pm. He will also give a solo recital of music connected with his instrument. 'When this cello came into my hands in 1979,' he says on the phone from his home in Mexico City, 'I thought I would like to find out something about its history. Then, I can say, it turned into some kind of obsession. I became a detective investigating the life of a cello.'

"It wasn't an easy task; musical instruments often leave no trace in history. 'It has taken me 10 years, and visits to countless museums, cathedrals, and places where the cello has been,' Prieto says.

"Known as the 'red cello' because of its warmly glowing varnish, the Piatti cello was made in 1720 - around the time when Bach was writing his six extraordinary suites for unaccompanied cello. Besides the Piatti, the 76-year-old master luthier from Cremona, Antonio Stradivari, produced 14 violins that year. It took him just over a month to make the cello from Balkan maple and Italian pine.

"'Once finished,' writes Prieto, 'it was hung in front of a large window in his workshop so that the sun would dry the marvellous varnish.' Prieto envisages his cello's biography as a series of journeys. It stayed at Stradivari's house until after the instrument-maker's death, when a cellist named Carlo Moro bought it from one of the Stradivari sons.

"In 1762 Moro and some other musicians from Cremona were offered jobs with an opera orchestra in southern Spain. They crammed into a coach, with the cello in a wooden box on the top rack along with the rest of the baggage, and set off. Moro and his cello worked at the opera house in Cadiz until 1773, when the opera company packed up, leaving Moro without a source of income.

"He was, however, fortunate in his friends. One of them was Father Jose Saenz de Santa Maria, a fiercely determined priest who not only got Moro a job with the cathedral orchestra but also, in 1786, managed to commission the most famous composer in Europe at the time, Franz Josef Haydn, to write a liturgical piece for a regular passiontide rite in a local cave. And so it was that the first documented concert by the Piatti was on Good Friday 1787 in the Santa Cueva de Cadiz, at the premiere of Haydn's *The Seven Last Words of our Saviour on the Cross.*

"By 1818 the cello had come into the hands of Allen Dowell, an Irish wine merchant and violinist based in Cadiz. Known as 'Don Alonso Dowell', he seems to have been something of a Del Boy - a contractor for the British army, he also enjoyed trading in top-notch musical instruments, which he bought for a song in Spain, then sold in England for a tasty profit.

"In 1818 he returned to Ireland, bringing the Piatti cello with him. After his death it was bought by a clergyman and amateur cellist from Carlow, the Reverend Booth, and in 1867 it became the property of the man whose name it now bears, the Italian cellist Alfredo Piatti.

"HAPPY EVER AFTER? Not quite. In another picaresque twist the cello ended up in Nazi Germany in the hands of Francesco Mendelssohn, whose father was a nephew of composer Felix Mendelssohn. He managed to smuggle it across the border into Switzerland - on his bicycle - and thence to New York. Sadly, once there he went into a downward spiral of alcoholism; with some hair-raising results for the Piatti, which was often left behind in bars by way of settling the tab.

"One night after a concert, Mendelssohn had a few scoops too many and, on getting out of a taxi on East 62nd Street, was unable to open his own front door. Gradually it dawned on him that he was at the wrong house. Leaving the cello case on the footpath, he staggered off in search of the right one. Next morning he woke to hear his housekeeper declaring, 'Isn't this your cello? I found it lying in the street just as the garbage truck was about to pick it up. . .'

"Francesco Mendelssohn died in 1971, leaving the cello to the Marlboro Foundation which, in 1978, decided to sell it. It was bought at last by one Carlos Prieto. Not to be outdone by his illustrious predecessors, the cello's 20th-century owner adds a clutch of entertaining anecdotes of his own, including tales from his trips to China, India and Russia - a flight to Tbilisi, in Georgia, is described in spine-tingling detail - and, for good measure, adds a section on the history of instrument-making plus another on cello music from 1700 to the present day.

"It's the latter that - apart from his cello - interests the 71-year-old Prieto more than anything else. He has made it his business to promote the work of contemporary Latin American composers, and is a tireless commissioner of new music, including a cello concerto by John Kinsella.

"'I am sometimes accused of adopting a quixotic attitude, of fighting a losing battle,' he writes in his book. 'However, I am inspired by the relentless quest for the masterpieces of the future. If even a small fraction of these works manages to survive, I will be extremely satisfied.'

"The CD that accompanies the book is a showcase for this aspect of his musical life. On it, Prieto performs a selection of strikingly varied pieces for solo cello, two cellos, cello and piano and cello and chamber orchestra.

"These range from works by Astor Piazzolla and Manuel de Falla to music by Mexican composers in the shape of Mario Lavista's *Three Secular Dances*, a delicate evocation of the courtship rituals of imaginary birds, and Samuel Zyman's melodic *Suite for Two Cellos*, commissioned jointly by Prieto and Yo-Yo Ma.

"His solo recital in Dublin will feature three movements from Zyman's *Suite for Cello Solo*, four movements from Bach's *Suite in C Major*, and the world premiere of a new short piece, *Una Giga Para Carlos (A Jig For Carlos)*, by John Kinsella. And it will bring the Piatti back, once again, to where it lived for more than 30 years. Does it enjoy its visits here? 'I'm sure the cello loves coming back to Ireland,' Prieto says. 'I certainly do.'

"Carlos Prieto will play at the John Field Room of the NCH on Feb 4 at 8pm. Adventures of a Cello is published by University of Texas Press, $24.95"[50]

AN EXPERT'S ANALYSIS OF BOOK AND PLAY BY DAVID FULTON

FRED WURLITZER <franwurlit2@gmail.com>   7-1- 2020

to David

I'm exhausted and you are still going. Impressive.

My assumption is that Tarisio records for 40316 and 51374 are at least partially correct. If so, they substantiate my father's story no matter what stock cards may or may not say.

You wrote,
"Also, to my amazement, they took only a total of 197 Stradivari instruments altogether into inventory. Those, of course, were the Strads that were on consignment to be sold. I am certain Rembert certified lots of others and that is a gross underestimate of how many Stradivari instruments he examined. But only 197 were ever in inventory, and that's a

---

[50] Memoirs of a Stradivarius Piatti Cello. Jan 29, 2008. *Irish Times*. This episode has been well documented. https://www.irishtimes.com/culture/memoirs-of-a-stradivarius-1.932980 June 30, 2020.

solid figure."

I am amazed. The 135 number I came up with is almost irrelevant if the 197 number applies to violins, except to reinforce that records, at least those of Goodkind and Tarisio, are nearly totally inadequate as published. I am going to have a stiff drink. But you wrote "197 Stradivari instruments." How many of those were violins? The 135 number I give is for violins only.

Your scholarship and eagerness to solve a puzzle, that is, what was the red violin my father reported Rembert found, is endearing. I feel Tarisio, despite their inaccuracies, has reported some truth.   I think it is a mistake to rely totally on stock cards. Where did Tarisio get its information that substantiates my father's story? I certainly didn't create the Tarisio renditions. They came from somewhere. They did not arise de novo as a neoplasm. They did not arise in my imagination. Stock cards do not in the least explain the Tarisio renditions. A reasonable conclusion is that in the case of The Mendelssohn stock cards are incomplete, because the *Mendelssohn* stock card was never filed. Rembert didn't care. How do you explain the discrepancies between the Tarisio renditions and Rembert's stock cards? You know my answer. What is yours? My sense is that you are not afraid or disconcerted being challenged by me.

Your diligence and professionalism are heart-warming. You are a scholar hard in pursuit of truths. You seem to have more energy than I have.

I trust you will find the play entertaining. It is, of course, based upon considerable poetic license and speculation. It needs cutting and editing. Perhaps, some day it will be produced.

Thanks, thanks.
Fred

David Fulton   7-1-2020
to me

Fred,

Here's the stock card breakdown:

   158 Violins
     3 Violas
    16 Cellos
    19 Labels – probably photographs of labels of some of the Strads they did not take into inventory but, perhaps, certified
     1 Blank – used to add instruments to the database, not an instrument
    ------
   197

So there are actually 197 Stradivari instruments that are represented in the stock cards. I think it would be fair to add the labels to the list, not as inventoried instruments but as instruments examined by Rembert and, quite probably, certified. I shouldn't be surprised if the label that appears in the 1720 Strad listing is, in fact, the label of the Mendelssohn Strad.

I don't think you could make your case vis-à-vis the Red Violin in a court of law. But I think you have plenty of framework to hang your story on.

Energy level: Well, I'm only 76 after all. You're 7 years older so you have a good excuse.

MY REPLY 7-2-2020:

I agree I may not have enough evidence to definitely convince a jury. But I wouldn't bet on that assumption and the question still remains: Where did Tarisio get the records for 40316 and 51374 that strongly suggest, once one knows they are the same violin, that my father's story is true. I suggest respectfully Tarisio is not totally wrong. I suggest it is a mistake to rely totally on Rembert's stock cards. I suggest again and again Rembert had no incentive to register the red violin my father said he found. I cannot conclusively prove Rembert found a red violin or that the red violin was The Mendelssohn, but the circumstantial including my father's story, Rembert's early appointment at the age of 22 in 1926 to be appointed head of acquisitions based in part possibly on having found a red Stradivarius, and recorded Tarisio evidence is impressive. Nor have you been able to disprove the story.

Unfortunately, there are no surviving Wurlitzer or Hamma records to support or disprove the story that Rembert found a red Strad. There is only the evidence I have already presented. That evidence would probably convince a jury IMO.

Anyway, the main thrust of the book was to support the play that I would like to see produced some day. I suspect the play is highly accurate. The lack of evidence in the stock cards, I respectfully suggest, is a red herring.

Your help has been significant. I acknowledge you repeatedly in the book and play. I am appreciative.

I would like to add your last Email as a post-script at the end of the book -- or at least consider adding it.

Stock cards are very important, but please don't discount other evidence. A court of law might place unusual emphasis on the Tarisio records that support my father's story. It would be a mistake to prejudge how a jury would decide. If a judge ruled in favor of my father's story, would that really matter? Why not submit the arguments to dealers and violin experts? I could prepare a brief that they would review on and rule. That might be entertaining.

Best regards,

Fred

David Fulton   7-2-2020
to me

Fred,

All the instruments were Stradivaris. Each and every one. I could, if pressed, list them all for you though that would be burdensome. All are Strads and that you can take to the bank.

David

FRED WURLITZER   7-2-2020
to David

CONCLUSIONS: The list of 135 violin Strads Rembert or a Wurlitzer handled can be expanded to a minimum of 158. The Story of Rembert finding a red Strad has not been disproven. Nor has the story been absolutely proven. Because considerable evidence exists that Rembert did discover a red Strad, there is sufficient evidence to support one heck of a play.

May I have your permission to quote your figures?

Fred

David Fulton   7-2-2020

to me

Fred,

Yes, by all means note that the Wurlitzer records prove that they
handled at least 158 Stradivari violins, 3 Strad violas (a very big
deal, there are only 11 in existence), and 15 Strad cellos. That is rock
solid. It would be possible to produce stock cards images for all
those instruments.

David

Addendum III

Introduction to *Rembert,* the Play

CHARACTERS

Principal Characters

- **REMBERT**, a famous American violin collector and dealer;
- **RUDOLPH** Henry, Rembert's father and also a famous American expert in rare violins;
- **HERR HAMMA,** a well-known German violin dealer and Wurlitzer colleague in Stuttgart;
- **RAIMUND**, the first cousin of Rembert;
- **LEE**, Rembert's wife;
- **VIRGINIA**, a sexy, young woman.
- **FRANCESCO,** grand nephew of Felix Mendelssohn.

Minor Characters

- **GYPSY,** who plays a red violin to recorded music;
- **POLICE OFFICER**, a local police officer;
- **REPORTER,** a newspaper reporter;

Note: One actor plays **HERR HAMMA**, the **GYPSY**, and the **POLICE OFFICER.** Another actor plays the **REPORTER and FRANCESCO**. Different actors play **REMBERT, RUDOLPH,** and **RAIMUND**. One actress can also play the roles of both **LEE** and **VIRGINIA**, or there can be two actresses. There are a total of ten characters, but possibly only six or seven actors, depending upon how the Director assigns roles.

This is the author's first play.

PLOT

This is a play about Rembert, who discovered a red Stradivarius violin, later known as *The Red Violin* or *The Mendelssohn*. Rembert and his father Rudolph Henry became two of the world's greatest dealers and sellers, usually on consignment of Stradivari violins – an amazing 158 Stradivari violins in total. That record includes 39 Stradivari violins sold by him and his father Rudolph through The Wurlitzer Music Company.

Most of the Stradivaris sold by a Wurlitzer were by Rembert later through his world-famous company, The Rembert Wurlitzer Company, which Rembert founded in 1949 and located it originally on 42nd Street in New York City.

The story starts with Rembert and his dad, Rudolph, in an office (Scene #1), where they talk about the beauty of Stradivari violins and the remarkable 300-year family history (today, it is a 400-year history) of making musical instruments. Scenes #2 through #5 are at an outdoor Berlin café where Rembert first identifies an unknown red violin. Scenes #6 and #7 are like Scene #1, located in an office. There are then essentially just two set designs.

The plot develops in large part from a story the author's father Raimund told him several times about how he was with Rembert when he discovered a red Stradivarius violin in Berlin. The author's father never mentioned the year this event took place, but presumably it was sometime before he resigned in late 1928. Raimund's recitation was not hearsay.

The book by the author Fred Wurlitzer available on Amazon.com as *The Real Red Violin* recites this story. Rembert is shown as a gifted young man who is totally infatuated and obsessed with rare violins. Fortunately, he discovers a red Stradivarius that in the play becomes a major focus of his life. His father forces him to sell it. He recovers it. He hides it. He then possesses it again until he dies.

Raimund, a character in this play, is the father of the author, and Rembert is the first cousin once removed of the author. Howard is the grandfather of the author and CEO of Wurlitzer, while Rudolph is the great uncle of the author and head of the rare instruments department. Rudolph, Howard, and Farny are brothers who are sons of Franz Rudolph, the founder of the Wurlitzer Music Company. The author feels free to write about his father, Rembert, and his wife Lee, since they have all died.

FAMILY TREE

To help the audience understand relationships, a family tree follows that outlines the filial relations of the principal characters in this mostly true-to-life play.

This outline can be put in the program. The author apologizes for the convoluted family connections, although they are what they are.

Wurlitzer Family Tree

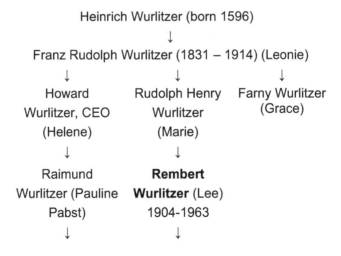

Heinrich Wurlitzer (born 1596)
↓
Franz Rudolph Wurlitzer (1831 – 1914) (Leonie)

↓	↓	↓
Howard Wurlitzer, CEO (Helene)	Rudolph Henry Wurlitzer (Marie)	Farny Wurlitzer (Grace)
↓	↓	
Raimund Wurlitzer (Pauline Pabst)	**Rembert Wurlitzer** (Lee) 1904-1963	
↓	↓	

Frederick Wurlitzer, M.D.(Author)	Marianne Wurlitzer	Rudy Wurlitzer

Henry Farny, the painter, was the brother of Leonie.

This play follows logical speculations about what conversations actually took place over time by the author's family members a long time ago. This play is not entirely a fairy tale. Mostly what is related is based on facts as the author could find them looking at databases, reading numerous books, and communicating with relatives and associates.

A central theme in the play is the search for beauty. Stradivari violins are works of art. Searching for them and then possessing them gives Rembert satisfaction. Rembert is described as having a fetish for rare violins with an Oedipal-complex overlay.

His greatest moment comes when at the age of 26 he discovers a red Stradivarius violin. In recognition of the knowledge he demonstrated by recognizing an unknown Stradivarius, the Wurlitzer Board appoints him head of acquisitions. That violin becomes a major part of his life.

A second theme is that of the love-hate relationships between fathers and sons. The relationship between father Rudolph and son Rembert is not smooth. Nor is the relationship between Raimund and his father Howard tranquil. The parallels between Rembert and Raimund and their fathers mirror the double-helical strand structure of DNA twisting and turning together or two grapevines twisting together as they mature. Curious psychological parallels coexist between the two main "R" characters, Rembert and Raimund.

Quantum entanglement may explain some opposites that coexist, like Schrödinger's Cat or predestination with free will.[51] Saint Paul, if alive today, might affirm entanglements follow God's designs for order. Love-and-hate, have-and-have-not, and pride-with-humility relationships are co-existing psychological dualities that are often entangled.

Freud explained psychological entanglements differently from Saint Paul. Freud's emphasis was on the genitals, not God. As the author clarifies entangled conflicts from a Freudian point of view, his play becomes, in part, a psychodrama. Psychiatric issues are briefly explored, including the Freudian basis for understanding a fetish, love-hate, have versus have-not relationships, and the Oedipal Complex with son in conflict with father. Some of these themes are timeless. No doubt, if Rembert were alive, he would be amused at the Freudian overlays that the author suggests involved him.

Rembert is presented as being a bit of a spoiled brat when young. Rembert gets away repeatedly with challenging his father. Finally, he understands that he has always wanted to displace his father to be with his mother. When that insight occurs, his dreams are no longer the same. He is psychologically cured.

Don't be alarmed. Diversions to Freudian sexual analysis are interspersed purposely with dry, pedantic dissertations on Stradivari violins. There is room to breathe and relax. Sexual double entendres and sexual references will not overwhelm the reader or viewer. The author who is still a board-certified physician became fascinated with Freudian jargon two generations ago.

---

[51] Predestination coexisting with free will is a frequent theme in the New Testament. The author has written extensively about this paradox in his book *Love to the Trinity* that is availble on Amazon.com.

A minor, almost irrelevant theme, is that it may be difficult, often in the absence of provenance, to prove a rare, old violin is a Stradivarius.

There are Wurlitzers making music instruments still today. That equates to there being now over a remarkable four-hundred-year lineage of Wurlitzer musical instrument-making. How one might explain this longevity in focus is another theme. The American Wurlitzer Music Company itself is out of business, although there is a Deutsche Wurlitzer making instruments in Hűllhorst.

The author is a black sheep who decided to become a physician instead of becoming a Wurlitzer instrument maker. There was a brief period though when he was able to appoint a surrogate to the Wurlitzer Board.

In writing the play, characters start speaking a few words in German. The author asks that the actors do the same in order to add authenticity to the well-defined German ancestry and very extensive German business relations of the principals.

Who has ever read a play with footnotes? In this play, they are used liberally as proofs of authenticity for background. I trust they will not distract the actors from following the lines. If they do bother the actors, just remove them. The author does not expect the footnotes to be read or made available to an audience unless they buy the book. They are meant to give actors oomph and sometimes direction in understanding better the author's thoughts when writing the play.

After reading and seeing the play, one may learn more about Stradivari violins that one ever thought possible. Hopefully, the reader and the audience will gain a better understanding of what beauty is and understand better psychological relationships evident throughout humanity.

Oedipus Rex was written almost 2,500 years ago. It has always been one of the author's favorite plays. Parallels with *Rex* in this play are not accidental.

In writing this play, the author had a dilemma. It was a burden. How could he make a play just about violins interesting?

The author thought of deleting many verbal exchanges about violins. Then after asking his wife and a friend whether he should do that, they reassured him. They said no, those exchanges were interesting.

An interesting character in the play is Francesco Mendelssohn, the grand nephew of Felix Mendelssohn. In a famous episode around 1950, Francesco left the famous Stradivarius *Piatti Cello* on a sidewalk as he staggered from one house to another seeking his home. In the play, he loses *The Mendelssohn* in a drunken stupor in Berlin in 1913. Just as others reported he would leave the *Piatti* in bars in New York to ensure payment,[52] so the author imagines he left *The Mendelssohn* on the street in Berlin in 1913 to ensure payment to a trash taker who then sold the violin to a gypsy. Well, truth can be stranger than fiction and sometimes fiction the same as truth.

In writing a play or a book, a dedication or an acknowledgment is appropriate. Without the benefit of having been confined because of the Coronavirus, the author would never have had the patience and focus to write this play.

Finally, after this extensive introduction, we can get to the play itself. Thanks for having been patient.

---

[52] https://www.irishtimes.com/culture/memoirs-of-a-stradivarius-1.932980

Addendum IV
OPENING

The actor playing Francesco Mendelssohn enters, faces the audience, and states his thoughts. He is dressed as a Jew with a skull cap – and he is drinking from a bottle of whiskey labeled in bold letter "WHISKEY."

FRANCESCO   I am Francesco Mendelssohn; I am truly a clod. My great uncle, Felix, was truly a genius. He was not a clod. His music was glorious, almost as ethereal as the music of Bach. I am such a drunken fool. I've lost Felix's violin, *The Mendelssohn*. He would play the Chaconne on it. It was heaven opening its heart to all men. I am leaving to have another drink.

[Francesco staggers off the stage when he finishes his sad opening soliloquy.]

Rembert, The Play

SCENE 1

A den filled with books and violins where Rudolph is sitting behind a desk. A sign high above the desk says, "Wurlitzer Music Company" and immediately below that there is "Cincinnati." The year is 1922 when Rembert is 18 years old.

[Rembert knocks on the door]

RUDOLPH   Come in.

[Rembert enters.]

You're late. Still, it's good to see you, son. Sit down, please. Have you been enjoying Cincinnati? Your mother and I missed you today.

REMBERT   Yes, Dad, I enjoyed my time in New York visiting dealers, but I missed Mom and you too.

RUDOLPH   You just got back home, and we didn't see you. What did you do today that was so important that you couldn't have spent time first with us?

REMBERT   I went to the Cincinnati Art Museum to see my Uncle Henry Farny's paintings again. He really was a great Western artist, better in my mind than Remington or Russell.[53] He didn't care what people thought of him. He only cared about painting. He told me it was important to do what you like. "Be your own guide. Look

---

[53] Henry Farny was the brother of Leonie, wife of Franz Rudolph the founder of Wurlitzer. His paintings usually sell for over a million dollars today. His works are in The Metropolitan Museum of Art, the Kimbell Art Museum in Ft. Worth and other major art museums. President Teddy Roosevelt, a personal friend, once told Farny the nation owed him a great debt, because of his portrayals of Indian life. Farny Wurlitzer was a different Farny who was the brother of Howard and Rudolph Henry.

for beauty," he told me. I miss him and his simplicity and purity of focus.

RUDOLPH   Don't distract me. What do you want to do? Most importantly, how are you doing?

REMBERT   I wasn't trying to distract you. You asked me what I want to do when I feel you really don't care. You want me to go to university. I don't. I want to study violins. I want to find beauty, not just in a woman.

RUDOLPH   You're certainly abrupt and to the point. Okay, I'll put aside your directness. Why is there always tension between us? So, let's talk now about you, not Farny.

[A pause as Rudolph reflects]

Son, you have always been very special to me, not just because you are my only son, but because of your love for violins. That love reminds me of myself. I think you should go to university and then come and work with Howard and me. Then, you can pursue your love affair of fine violins. How you developed that love, I'm not sure.

REMBERT   It was from you, Dad, that I developed my love for violins. You were an excellent violinist yourself. You even studied under Emanuel Wirth in Berlin for almost a year. Your deep love for rare violins somehow struck a musical chord in my soul. I just responded with love myself, almost as strong as my love for my mother.[54] We share a love for the beauty of rare violins and Mom.

RUDOLPH   Those are wonderful sentiments.

REMBERT   Dad, I really appreciate your kindness and support, but I just do not see how university will help me. I wonder what I will learn and if what I learn will help me. I love violins and playing them[55] more than I do women. I just want to know everything about them like you. I'm angry that I have to go to Princeton.

RUDOLPH   University will help you broaden your knowledge. It will introduce you to new ideas, maybe even different women other than your mom.

REMBERT   You didn't go to university and neither did your brothers Farny and Howard. My grandfather Franz Rudolph thought university was a waste of time,[56] and so did you. I really don't like being forced to do what none of my family did. Why are you doing this?

RUDOLPH   I regret now I didn't go to university. I want the best for you. I understand your feelings, even if I do not sympathize with your priorities like

---

[54] This is the first hint of an Oedipal Complex.

[55] This is another obvious sexual hint.

[56] *Wurlitzer Family History* by Lloyd Graham 1955. Page 51

going to the art museum here in Cincinnati before seeing your mother and me. Frankly, I insist you go to university. Let's have no more talk that you won't go.

REMBERT   I regret I didn't see Mom first. How could I have seen Mom without seeing you? You are putting me in a can. You're squeezing me into a tube. I feel like I am in a vise.[57] You are tormenting me.

RUDOLPH   You're mixing metaphors, son.

REMBERT   To hell with mixed metaphors! Please try to understand me. I guess I was blessed, or maybe cursed, with an orientation that violins are the greatest. I even think more about violins than I do about women and sex or even Mom.

RUDOLPH   That's really weird. Maybe, my friend Sigmund Freud would say you have a fetish or a lust for violins. After all, violins have hourglass figures. He would say if you understood your dreams, you would understand yourself better.

REMBERT   Really?

RUDOLPH   Yes, really! I can arrange an appointment with Herr Freud if you are even a little bit interested. As you apparently know, Sigmund played

---

[57] "I hate and yet love. You may wonder how I manage it. I don't know, but feel it happen, and am in torment". The ancient Roman writer Catullus introduced the love–hate theme into Western culture with these famous lines.

music on a Wurlitzer piano.[58] I sold one to him a while back. He played it for me in his home on Bergasse not far from our home on Wurlitzergasse[59] in Vienna. You may be amused that I once told him I dreamed of violins, but he just smiled and said nothing more. So, I prefer not saying anything more. I don't think Freud wanted to challenge me, since he wanted to buy one of our pianos.

REMBERT How anyone would see my love for violins as being erotic is beyond my understanding, I just dream of their beauty.[60] Some men dream of naked women. Not I!

RUDOLPH Yes, I do feel your love for violins is erotic.

[Suddenly, there is knocking on the closed door of the den. Rudolph says enter, and a gorgeous well-endowed young Madame, a Dolly Parton type with a low-cut blouse showing her breasts, enters with her hips swaying. She is a caricature of a sexual bombshell.]

---

[58] Burke,Fanine. *The Sphinx on the Table: Sigmund Freud's Art Collections and the Development of Psychoanalysis.* A Wurlitzer piano is listed in the inventory of items owned by Sigmund Freud. Presumably, Rudolph sold him this piano. Playing music on a piano is another Freudian association with sex.

[59] Wurlitzergasse is a well-known alley or lane in Vienna where Wurlitzers lived not far from where Freud lived. Wikipedia. Raimund once mentioned to the author he had met Freud.

[60] One of Freud's definitive works was *The Interpretation of Dreams.*

VIRGINIA	Hello, Mr. Wurlitzer. Your wife Marie told me to knock and enter. Excuse me for interrupting your meeting with Rembert. I had to see him to tell him that I can see him tonight at the theater.
RUDOLPH	Come in Virginia. Have a seat. Rembert has told me about you. He didn't say, however, how beautiful you are.
REMBERT	She's gorgeous! Virginia,
	[Rembert looks at Virginia with wide, exaggerated, adoring eyes.]
	I'll pick you up before the theater. We'll go for drinks afterwards and maybe more fun later.
VIRGINIA	Okay, sweetie. I'll see you anon.
REMBERT	No, sweetheart, please stay. Protect me from my dad.
VIRGINIA	You're a big boy. You can protect yourself.
REMBERT	Please stay. He's going to tell me again about family history. You've wanted to know it. I've been reluctant to tell it. So, here's your chance.
RUDOLPH	Yes, please stay, Virginia. You can give me an excuse to hit Rembert over the head again by

emphasizing once more to him how important our history should be to us.[61]

VIRGINIA   Okay, I'll stay. But I don't want to get into the midst of an argument between the two of you. If things get heated, I'll leave.

RUDOLPH   Okay, that's a deal. You can be our arbitrator.

VIRGINIA   I agree.

RUDOLPH   Don't patronize me, son. I don't like your tone of resentment. At risk of boring you further and putting you to sleep again, I insist on discussing a mystery about longevity with Virginia. Be patient. I am talking to Virginia, not to you. I'll start with our ancestor Heinrich Wurlitzer who was born in 1596. He started making violins and other musical instruments over three hundred years ago.[62] Frederick Wurlitzer was a child prodigy who toured Europe in concert presentations and who became the court pianist to Frederick the Great of Prussia at the age of sixteen.[63] Wurlitzers have been making and dealing with musical instruments ever since then. I expect Wurlitzers will be doing the same for another century or more. How can this be?

---

[61] A hint of sadism emerges.

[62] Fairfield, John. Known Violin Makers. 1942. Page 185. Frederick Wurlitzer became the namesake of the author.

[63] Ibid. The author's namesake was the court musician to Frederick the Great. The author has no aptitude for playing music. His favorite composer is Bach and his favorite music the Chaconne on a Stradivarius or a Bach Cantata on a Mighty Wurlitzr organ.

How does one explain this longevity in focus for hundreds of years? All this focus was possible too without a focus on sex.

VIRGINIA   That's so interesting!

[She says as she bends over showing her cleavage. Hopefully, the audience will also find her cleavage interesting. If this action bothers the director, just follow your instincts as to what an audience will accept. Maybe, women would be offended.]

I suspect the focus was on not on sex either. How could there be sex with a musical instrument?

[Her eyes are wide open suggesting innocence.]

REMBERT   Dad, I'm trying hard not to yell at you. This is such blarney about family history and university. You're just pretending to talk to Virginia.

RUDOLPH   You should be impressed and proud of our history. I suppose I have a degree of low self-esteem because I didn't go to university.

REMBERT   How is that relevant to my needs?

[Soliloquy #1]

[Soliloquys are numbered to give structure to the director and actor playing Rembert. Most soliloquys are interchangeable.

Delivered angrily]

Dad, I can't explain the mystery of a family focus for hundreds of years being involved one way or another with music. Maybe psychiatric illnesses are passed down genetically from one generation to the next.[64] Some genetic illnesses like hemophilia are certainly passed down for generations. Maybe, love-hate relationships between father and son are passed down culturally through generations. I recall Franz Rudolph, who founded our company, was divorced by his father Christian Gottfried. Christian passed the business in East Germany to his youngest, only six-year-old son, Constatin. Franz Rudolph bitterly resented what his father had done. Now I bitterly feel you are disinheriting me. You're pushing me to leave rare violins, although violins came first in your life. Disinheritance has flowed from fathers to sons in our family.[65] I would rather

---

[64] "Most psychiatric disorders are highly heritable; the estimated heritability for bipolar disorder, schizophrenia, and autism (80% or higher) is much higher than that of diseases like breast cancer and Parkinson disease." Wikipedia

[65] Franz Joseph's father disinherited him. Howard did not support his son Raimund with job promotions. Raimund's mother disinherited Raimund leaving her considerable fortune to charity. Raimund disinherited his children including the author. The author and his wife intend to bypass their children by giving their assets to charity.

	think about Virginia and beautiful violins than university. I would rather be with Virginia and violins than with you.[66]
VIRGINIA	Rembert, I said I would stay if matters did not become too intense. Apologize now to your father.
REMBERT	I'm sorry, Dad. I became angry.
RUDOLPH	Our conversations are always so tense. There's no doubt you do indeed have a lust for violins. Freud might call that lust a violin fetish.[67] It's curious that Freud suggested to me I had a lust for violins too. Everyone in our family fell in love with music one way or another. Everyone sought beauty somehow in what they did.

REMBERT

[Soliloquy #2]

[Again, delivered angrily]

Maybe God foreordained me to have an alliterative fetish[68] for violins, Virginia, and her vagina.[69] If I was foreordained, I still have

---

[66] Now Rembert is hinting at disinheriting or divorcing his dad. He left Wurlitzer a year after his father Rudolph died in 1948.

[67] "A fetish is a form of sexual desire in which gratification is linked to an abnormal degree to a particular object." Wikipedia. Rembert denies an erotic connection. Freud would disagree.

[68] At first "programmed" was used before predestined or foreordained, but then computer programming had not occurred yet at the time of this conversation.

[69] Phonological alliteration was explored by Freud.

free will.[70] Yet, I have no will to be away from her or violins. So, perhaps my lack of will to go to university was predestined. Maybe, each father affected every son by example. It then became the son's choice whether or not to follow the father. I don't know, and I don't care. I only know I lust for violins; I don't love Virginia. I like her body though. I lust for it. I'm not interested in psychoanalysis.

VIRGINIA Psychoanalysis might help you Rembert. You insult me talking about my vagina.

REMBERT I apologize.

RUDOLPH Be patient, son. Answers will emerge.

REMBERT Are you kidding? Be patient. Excuse me, what nonsense! I feel such ambivalence[71] towards you. I dislike intensely being pushed. It irritates me that I also love you. There's a strange entanglement when love and hate coexist. I feel

---

https://books.google.ca/books?id=kt6CDwAAQBAJ&pg=PA48&lpg=PA48&dq= alliteration+and+freud&source=bl&ots=xZOB0x9tAT&sig=ACfU3U2Szw2 PWlHgM3HxBGs6JVHGdScJGQ&hl=en&sa=X&ved=2ahUKEwiL2vaUhpj pAhXPrZ4KHS_GD5oQ6AEwA3oECAYQAQ#v=onepage&q=alliteration %20and%20freud&f=false

[70] Predestination coexisting with free will is a Christian complex tenet. Quantum entanglement allows opposites like particle/wave duality and predestination with free will to coexist.

[71] Ambivalence was the term borrowed by Sigmund Freud to indicate the simultaneous presence of love and hate towards the same object. Opposites co-exist throughout nature like yin and yang or love and hate.

no animosity in lusting for violins and Virginia. That lust is simple.

RUDOLPH   Why are you so angry?

REMBERT   I keep explaining why I'm angry. When all I want to talk about are violins, all you do is talk stubbornly about family history and university. I'm not interested in what you're saying. Can't you understand that? Maybe, you should talk to a psychiatrist. Maybe, I should too.

VIRGINIA   Yes, maybe the two of you should get help from a psychiatrist. And Rembert you are being rude.

RUDOLPH   Ha, Rembert, it's best that I ignore you. I prefer doing that to hitting you on the head with a hammer. Please understand I am talking to Virginia again, not you. After my father, Franz Rudolph, was disinherited, he immigrated to America. Here in Cincinnati he built a great business making musical instruments of all sorts. During the Civil War his profits were high making trumpets and drums for the Union Army. Now our company makes the Mighty Wurlitzer organs for movie theaters, and automated orchestrions and other automated musical instruments. Our name means music to millions of Americans.

VIRGINIA   That's really interesting. Now, it's time for me to leave. Thanks so much to the two of you for including me. I'll see you anon Rembert at the theater this evening

REMBERT   I'll pick you up. We can have drinks and fun later.

[Virginia exits with hips swaying]

RUDOLPH   What a bombshell! Wow! I've forgotten what I was saying. I've even forgotten what I was thinking.

REMBERT   Thank God. Maybe, you'll stop reciting family history. She reminds me of the Stradivarius called *The Virgin* or *La Pucelle* that I once played.[72] She's really a beauty, isn't she, Dad?

RUDOLPH   It amuses me we can agree she is beautiful. Then, let's talk about her more.

REMBERT   Okay.

RUDOLPH   Her name is Virginia. Is she a virgin?

REMBERT   Not anymore.

RUDOLPH   Does she know anything about playing a violin?

REMBERT   No, but she does know how to play my strings.

---

[72] Rembert loaned *La Pucelle* to the La Salle String Quartet in 1953 for a concert in Cincinnati. That was years later, so there is a time warp or poetic license being taken. Rembert bought *La Pucelle* in 1955 for $25,000. In 2019 the Fulton Foundation sold *La Pucelle* for $22 million.

RUDOLPH   Are you in love with her?

REMBERT   I am, in my shabby way.

RUDOLPH   What do you mean "shabby"?

REMBERT   I think of sex with her; I don't think of loving her. My relations with her are simple. When I lust, she answers. We have a beautifully simple relationship founded on lust, like my relationship with violins.

RUDOLPH   Do you really think sex is simple?

REMBERT

[Soliloquy #3]

Only if I don't get married like you. Don't underestimate Virginia. I'm just not enthused about talking with her. I suppose my relationship with her is shallow, one built on lust. My relationship with violins is not shallow, although my violin relationships are also built on lust.

RUDOLPH   Hmmm! I understand your infatuations with her. She's like possessing a beautiful violin. So, think instead about Virginia and university for a while more than violins. After university, you can go back to violins or even, if you want, only Virginia and her vagina. Please understand, I am asking you to consider priorities.

REMBERT   Dad, I'm tired and ready to check out. At university, I might not see Virginia. Then my life could become complicated.

RUDOLPH   Am I boring you?

REMBERT

[Soliloquy #4]

You're pontificating. With all due respect, the story of your father, Franz Joseph, reinforces the point of love-hate relationships and disinheritance being part of our family history. I wonder how your father disinherited you. Maybe, I'll learn patience in university. But it will not be from you. Yes, you are boringly pedantic, except when you mentioned the Mighty Wurlitzer organ. Speaking of that, I've had a "Mighty Wurlitzer organ" all my life. I use it when I daydream about Virginia.

RUDOLPH   Smart aleck!

[as he lowers his head and chuckles fondly]

You're rude, crude, and socially unacceptable. You've got a fiery temperament. Just don't be rude with others who might be less patient than I am when you talk about your "mighty organ." You've truly tested my patience.

REMBERT

[Rembert is really a spoiled brat lecturing his father.]

Frankly, I feel I have more patience than you, Dad. Pushing me to do what I don't want to do does not impress me as being a virtue indicating patience.

A mystery to me is why I love you so much. I certainly don't lust for you, so my love for you is not built on lust. If I have love for violins or Virginia, it is built on lust. Sometimes, I see the love and lust as being the same, a duality in all of us. I agree with Virginia. Maybe, we both need psychoanalysis. How do I explain my love for you?

RUDOLPH

You act like a spoiled brat.

SCENE 2

A four-year time lapse takes place. The year is 1926

Background: Goebbels was sent by Hitler in October 1926 to the German capital, Berlin, to be its Gauleiter. The police declared the Nazi Party illegal in Berlin and eventually banned Nazi speech throughout the entire German state of Prussia.

Lights are dimmed as an outdoor café is set up.

An outdoor café in Berlin, Germany in 1926. A sign says in German, *"Wir feiern 1926 mit Bier."* (We celebrate 1926 with beer.) Raimund and Rembert are drinking beer.

RAIMUND   *Wie geht's mein Vetter?* How are you doing, my cousin? It's been four years since I last saw you just before you left for Princeton. So much has happened, and the Nazi Party has just been banned, I hope forever.

REMBERT   *Doch fein, Danke, und Prost!*

                       [...as Rembert lifts a stein of beer to Raimund who is also drinking beer, in fact, Pabst beer even though Pabst beer was unavailable in Germany at that time. The beer they are drinking can be labeled boldly "Pabst." They talk further in English.]

                       Very well, thank you, and *Prost.* Did you just get here? What are you doing here in Berlin?

I'm just fine; I'm here because I was bloody tired of university. So, I came to Berlin to drink beer and learn. I even have time to think about women and sex – and yes, the Nazis are being put down, fortunately.

RAIMUND   It's commendable that you would drink beer while learning and thinking about women and sex, when not worrying about Nazis. My wife Pauline and I were already in Germany. We have just come from Markneukirchen and Vienna where we visited relatives. So, it was easy for us to see you. My wife is back at our hotel.

REMBERT   I hope I can see Pauline later.

RAIMUND   Thank you. Maybe, we can get together later. So, fill me in, please. What's been happening in your life?

REMBERT

Soliloquy #5

[Related calmly]

As you know, I dropped out of Princeton after two years. I couldn't take it anymore.[73] I was angry with my father, who, in my mind, had forced me to attend. My father was deeply

---

[73] Bill Gates dropped out of Harvard. He couldn't take it anymore.

disappointed, but I don't feel I was a failure as he seemed to think I was. I just wasn't learning what I wanted to know. I was tired of studying what I didn't want to learn. So, I went to Europe, finally, at my father's suggestion after I had wasted two years. Here in Berlin, I visited numerous violin dealers and just talked with them about rare violins. It was illuminating. Actually, it was thrilling. I also went to France and Italy, where I studied violins and met violin dealers. Those two years were like a two-year postgraduate course in violins. Everyone welcomed me because of my father. No one wanted to talk about Nazis. I finally rationalized my anger at being made to go to university. I forgave my father.

RAIMUND   How did your father make you go to university?

REMBERT   He made it clear I better conform, or he wouldn't let me work with him later at Wurlitzer.[74] It was extortion.

RAIMUND   I know what you mean being upset with your father. Howard was very dominating with me. He made me go to university also. I didn't want to go. But I met my wife at university. So, it worked out okay. Howard insisted I do this and that, like going to his spy school where he

---

[74] The Wurlitzer Music Compay listed at one time on the NYSE as "Wurlitzer." Wurlitzer went out of business.

tested my memory. He would take me into a pub, leave, and then demand to know who had been in the bar, how they were dressed, and what they were talking about listening from a distance. I inevitably failed. It was weird.[75] He had other memory games. I resented them. Then, he demanded I work with him. I thought if I worked with him, he would abuse me more, and he did.

REMBERT   Maybe, it's a German thing to pressure children to carry on an inheritance.

RAIMUND   My wife and I will try not to influence our children excessively to do what we think they should do.

REMBERT   We have interesting parallels.[76] Our histories are like two grape vines twisting together as they grow[77], waiting to be plucked by others.

RAIMUND   Your father is very well known as an expert in rare violins. He has bought, authenticated, restored, and sold many, many Stradivari

---

[75] The author relates that his father, Raimund, often told him this story about what Raimund facetiously called his father Howard's "spy school." Howard had an eidetic memory. This "spy school" stuff is admittedly weird.

[76] Double parallels are like the helical structure of DNA. Of course, Watson and Crick discovered the helical structure of DNA well after this exchange the author will date to 1926. But the author finds the structure entertaining. Twists and turns between Rembert and Raimund occur time and time again, like DNA strands twisting and turning or two wine vines twisting and turning while maturing.

[77] DNA structure had not been discovered yet in 1926, but the parallel with two vines twisting together is evident.

instruments. You can be proud of him, and I know him to be well-intentioned. My father was well-intentioned too, but overbearing and impatient with incompetency. He thought I was incompetent.

REMBERT   Yes, my father is very well known, and he helped me tremendously with contacts. In England, I worked and studied with the very important English dealer and scholar, Mr. W.H. Hill, who offered me a job that I intend to turn down respectfully.[78] My father has worked often with Mr. Hill. He would be upset if I accepted a job from him. Now I just want to go back home to work in the violin department of our company.

RAIMUND   I hope when you return you don't feel you are entering enemy territory. Rembert, your father and I know that Mr. Hill offered you a job. Howard also knows, of course. Howard will protect you. He sees you as a son, more, I think, than he does me. I envy you. How can there be envy unless there is love?

[*A pause as Raimund reflects*]

Your father and Howard have tremendous admiration for you. Their job offer is one of the

---

[78] W.H. Hill and Wurlitzer connections were profound. Numerous correspondences between them still exist today. It probably disturbed Howard, Wurlitzer's CEO, that Hill tried to hire Rembert away. Offering Rembert an important job was probably seen as a counter-punch.

reasons I am here drinking beer with you. Pauline and I were here anyway in Germany. At the urging of your dad and my dad, my mission became to talk with you. All of us are concerned that you might reconsider Mr. Hill's offer. His offer, though, was quite a compliment.

REMBERT   Don't be concerned. I am very pleased your wife and you are here.

RAIMUND   Our friends and colleagues who are violin dealers in Berlin have already attested that you have a profound knowledge of and an unusual interest in rare violins. Mr. Hamma, our colleague, also attests to your abilities. Mr. Hill has confirmed your abilities, as evidenced by his job offer. We sincerely want you with us, not Mr. Hill.

REMBERT   Thank you for your kind comments. What do you have in mind?

RAIMUND   I am not just being kind; I am being truthful. We would very much welcome you back. Howard wants you. We run a family business that is on the New York Stock Exchange. We all recognize that we need someone like you.

We want you to return home to become head of Wurlitzer rare instrument acquisitions.[79]

REMBERT   What do Howard and my father say?

RAIMUND   The Board concurs that you will be put in charge of all instrument purchases, provided you are still interested. Consider what I'm saying as a job offer. We will talk about salary later, but you can be assured it will be fair. Your focus is most unusual. It is most uncommon as well for a major New York Stock Exchange company like Wurlitzer to offer such a prestigious position to a twenty-two-year-old.[80]

REMBERT   My focus on violins is like that of my father. Thank you, Raimund. If truth be known, I delayed responding to Mr. Hill because I felt in meeting with you, there might be a better job offer than his. I'll let you know after I talk with my dad. It's not just the money; it's the thought

---

[79] Rembert became head of rare violin purchases at Wurlitzer in 1926. He formed his own company, Rembert Wurlitzer, in 1948.

[80] Rembert was born in 1904. *The Music Trades*, page 13, December 25, 1926 issue, confirms his appointment as head of Wurlitzer acquisitions at the age of 22. The play suggests this appointment was made in part to prevent Rembert from going to work with Mr. Hill. The play suggests further that the Wurlitzer Board appointment was confirmed further by Rembert having proven his expertise through the discovery of a red Stradivarius violin earlier in 1926. That discovery comes shortly in the play.

of being with beautiful violins that really excites me.

RAIMUND   You have a sincere job offer. Do let us know soon if you are accepting the offer. I hope you are not saying that you would rather be with violins than with your dad. By the way, how is your German, please?

REMBERT   My German is pretty good now. Shall we speak in German?

RAIMUND   No, please. Let's continue to speak in English. Although my German is good, even still, I rarely have a chance to use it. After all my years in Cincinnati, I am now much more fluent in English. Learning German can be of great help, though, to a Wurlitzer. The Board did want to know how proficient you are in German, so we'll talk later *auf Deutsch*, my first language.[81]

REMBERT   I know German is important to be working for Wurlitzer, and I have been diligent. I can be of great help with our colleagues and relatives in Germany. I have met Fritz Wurlitzer, our "Clarinet Wurlitzer" in Erlbach, and Herr Hamma in Stuttgart several times.[82] I can help

---

[81] Although Raimund was born in Cincinnati, his first language was German. His parents, Howard and Helene, spoke German at home. He learned English in school. The author's mother, Paluline, sometimes spoke German at home with her husband Raimund.

[82] The author met the lady "Clarinet Wurlitzer" in Salzburg in 1998.

consolidate professional relations and not just family connections here in Germany.

RAIMUND   There is no doubt it really helps getting around Germany and Austria to speak fluent German. Our German connections are profound.

REMBERT   I also want to say that I appreciate and respect that you have come to Germany in large part just to offer me a job.

RAIMUND   Yes, but we did not come to Germany just to see you. Remember, please, we have relatives in Vienna on Wurlitzergasse. I was in Schöneck, and of course Markneukirchen, and then Vienna earlier seeing relatives and associates in the music business.

                     [A gypsy begins playing Bach's Chaconne outside where Raimund and Rembert are sitting.]

REMBERT   Stop talking, Raimund, for a moment, please. Do you hear that gypsy playing a violin?[83] I want to listen.

---

[83] The author's father related several times when the author was young that he had been present with Rembert in an outdoor café when he heard a gypsy playing a red violin that turned out to be a red Stradivarius. The author has no doubt his story of how Rembert found a red Stradivarius in Berlin in the late 1920s is true. Which red Stradivarius is still being debated. The author argues it was *The Mendelssohn*.

RAIMUND   Yes, of course. But so what? That's the Chaconne, and he's playing it well.

REMBERT   Hush! Listen!

[A five-second pause as Rembert listens raptly turning his head slowly side to side]

Oh, my God, I think he's playing a Stradivarius. I can't believe it.

RAIMUND   Are you sure?

REMBERT   Yes, I am almost sure. The sound is true, but I want to see the violin first before I am absolutely sure.

[Rembert goes up to the gypsy and politely asks...]

Hello mein Herr, darf Ich seine Geige ansehen? May I look at your violin?

GYPSY   *[With a heavy German accent]*

Naturlich. Spielen Sie die Geige? Naturally, do you play the violin?

REMBERT   *Jawohl, Ich kann die Geige spielen.* Yes, I can play the violin, but I don't want to play your violin now.[84] I just want to look at it. I think this is a very fine violin.

[Rembert looks intently at the violin turning it over several times, nodding his head up and down.]

I would like to buy it, please.

GYPSY   No, I don't want to sell it. You just walk up, and announce you want to buy my violin? Then you say you want to look at or play my violin.[85] Maybe, you were saying you want to play with my cock? You have *chutzpah* and big balls, my friend. But I will sell the violin to you anyway if you really have big balls for just $300. That's a bargain. I know you are American because of your *aussprache* or accent. And besides, all Americans have money. Do you have enough money?

REMBERT   Okay, I'll give you 1200 rentenmark, or, if you wish, 300 dollars. I have enough dollars with me to pay you right now. Just give me a handwritten receipt and don't ask to look at my balls.

GYPSY   Okay, take the violin. Thanks!

---

[84] Double entendre.
[85] Homosexuality was not at play with Rembert.

[The gypsy quickly scribbles out a receipt using Rembert's pen on a piece of scrap paper.]

I'll go and buy some schnapps. That would be more enjoyable than talking with you further about your balls and you playing mine.

REMBERT   *Geh mit Gott.* Go with God.

[Rembert goes back to the table outside the café.]

RAIMUND   You just bought that violin? That was quick. It sure is red in color.

REMBERT   Yes, I wanted it quick. That gypsy was very rude and crude – a real pain. I wanted to get away from him, if I could, quickly. Regarding the violin, I truly believe it's a red Stradivarius. I would like my father to authenticate it with me, then I can be absolutely sure. Anyway, it's a good violin, worth more than $300. If this is the violin I think it is, the mystery is who owned it before the gypsy.

RAIMUND   Getting your father involved might not be simple. He's in Cincinnati now. Let's go back to our hotels, and you can call him.

SCENE #3

Two weeks later, Rembert is again at the outdoor café, now with his father, Rudolph Henry. A sign is up as before, but now it just says "*Zwei Wochen später*" and underneath "Two weeks later." The year is still 1926.

Lights are dimmed and then turned up several times in the theater in order to accentuate this time-lapse of two weeks. The lights are red, of course, because this is a story, in part, about a red violin. Red is a color, also, for illicit sex. By the way, violins are not categorized by color.

REMBERT   Did you have a good trip, Dad? Was the cruise to Warnemunde[86] pleasant? I brought the red violin along so you can see it.

RUDOLPH   Yes, I had a good cruise. Your mother is not with me. I dropped all matters and came to Berlin as quickly as I could after you told me you had found a red Stradivarius. I wanted to see you and the Stradivarius. And more importantly, I wanted to confirm Raimund's job offer to head rare instrument purchases at Wurlitzer. Your appointment was based at first as a reaction to Mr. Hill's offer, but significantly confirmed later by the Wurlitzer Board upon the expertise you showed finding a red Stradivarius. I wanted to be sure you accept our job offer. We do not want to lose you to Mr.

---

[86] Warnemunde is the cruise port for Berlin.

Hill. Raimund told me you weren't sure and wanted to talk with me first.

REMBERT   Thanks, Dad. Your offer means a lot to me. I regret too if my leaving Princeton upset you.

RUDOLPH   Son, I am no longer offended you dropped out of university. What's your answer to our job offer?

REMBERT   Take matters in order, Dad. You used to be fond of lecturing me about priorities. May I suggest your first priority is to look at the violin? I am not being coy.

RUDOLPH   Okay, point well-made, Son. Let me play it so I can hear the sound.

[Rudolph plays a short passage of the Chaconne[87].]

Unbelievable! Yes, this is indeed a red Stradivarius. It even has the Stradivarius date of 1720 inside.

[Rudolph turns the violin over several times, looking at it intently.]

What a great find! You know, of course, how rare this violin is. What a coincidence it is that you of all people should be sitting at this same café when someone, you say a gypsy, started

---

[87] As mentioned earlier, Rudolph studied to be a concert violinist in Berlin.

playing a Stradivarius. Raimund wouldn't have known the difference. By the way, how did you know it was a gypsy?

REMBERT   Dad, I didn't know for sure he was a gypsy. He just looked like one.

RUDOLPH   Okay, he may have been my friend Fritz Kreisler in disguise.[88] Profiling can be unprofitable. But now, come on back with me to Cincinnati. Your find of a red Stradivarius truly impressed Howard and reassured him he made the right decision offering you a job. My confirmation that your find is indeed a red Stradivarius will reassure him further. He will have no doubts about you, even though you didn't stay at Princeton as he and I once insisted you do. You have been offered a very prestigious position at a very early age. You have proven your worth. Your future is bright.

REMBERT   Thanks again, Dad. I accept the job offer, and trust pay will be fair. Shall we take the violin back home?

RUDOLPH   No, I have another idea that I discussed with Howard and got his approval. Before leaving for home, I bet we can make a quick profit

---

[88] Rudolph and later Rembert knew almost all of the great violinists while they were alive including Heifitz, Hurwitz, Oistrakh, Menuhin, Milstein, Isaac Stern and many others. They came to Rembert's shop and Wurlitzer to look at and play great violins. Rembert would offer beer or wine, and even reluctantly water.

selling the violin to Hamma in Stuttgart. I will call him and see if he can join us quickly. We need to pay for our trip back home, and I'm joking, have change left over to buy beer. No, really, by offering the violin to Herr Hamma at a very reasonable price, we can consolidate our relations with him. He is a very important Wurlitzer colleague. Moreover, he is a dealer like W.H. Hill.[89] We must consolidate our relations with Mr. Hamma. So, with your permission, we'll invite him to join us at this beer garden and offer the violin to him for a very fair price.[90]

REMBERT   Dad, that sounds like bribery, but you always have a good sense of humor and feel for business. Have some beer before business, right? And we will have beer with Mr. Hamma, right? But can we just walk away from this violin? As an aside, how can a work of art as beautiful as this violin not have a provenance? It is like a lost Michelangelo sculpture in wood. It is a thing of beauty that has touched my soul.

---

[89] Hamma was Jewish. Hill was allegedly anti-anything not English and anti-Semetic. Hill's German was reportedly questionable. Rudolph and Rembert were not anti-Semetic.

[90] Mr. Hamma had long-time relations with W.H. Hill and Wurlitzer. There were also long-time relations between Wurlitzer and W.H. Hill. Wurlitzer and Hill were colleagues professionally, but competitors dealing in violins. Competition among the three was keen. Howard and the Wurlitzer Board would have felt a loss of prestige if Rembert accepted a job with W.H. Hill. That Rembert even delayed answering the job offer from Hill was seen by the Wurlitzer Board as a threat.

[Rembert nods his head slowly.]

RUDOLPH   When conducting business, drinking beer is smart. Beer loosens tongues and tension. Besides, you should be suspicious of anyone who says no when offered a free beer. Reliable people don't drink fruit juice. Mr. Hamma loves beer and he is reliable. Would you like a free beer?

I am amused and pleased to hear you waxing about a violin you just found. I promise you there will be many other Stradivari in your life. Maybe, there will be many other women too.

REMBERT   Yes, I agree. Teetotalers are a threat to world peace and good violin businesses.[91] We must always be suspicious of them.

Of course, you have my permission to sell my violin. I'm not your boss. I defer to you. We'll do what you want with my violin. I am annoyed, though, that you won't let me keep it. After all, it's mine; I used my own money to buy it. You are still my dad, demanding that I do what you want or what's good for Wurlitzer.

You are testing my loyalty. Yes, I'll have a beer, so you don't become suspicious of me. I'll drink beer every day from now on in order to

---

[91] Rembert is being sarcastic. He was not a cynical person. He makes this comment to appease his father. But actually his father is pretending to be cynical.

be reliable in your eyes. I won't accept Mr. Hill's offer. But at least allow me to keep any profits I make selling my violin at your command to Mr. Hamma.

[Another lapse occurs as the lights are dimmed again and three more days pass.

The Chaconne is again played.]

SCENE #4

The sign outside the café has changed once more, and says simply, almost poetically, rhyming in German, "*Zwei Tage später trinken Wir wieder Bier*" and underneath this is a sign that is not the least bit poetic, "Two Days Later We Drink Beer Again." The year is still 1926.

Herr Hamma is wearing lederhosen and has a pot belly. He is also wearing a funny Bavarian hat with a feather sticking out.

(Actually, Herr Hamma is not a Bavarian caricature who wears lederhosen and a funny Bavarian hat. He speaks Hochdeutsch and is from Stuttgart. Obviously, he's then rather formal and stilted. It's up to the director, not the author, whether or not to dress Herr Hamma in either a pin-striped suit, lederhosen, or some other attire. The author doesn't care. Mr. Hamma who is dead might have cared though.)

RUDOLPH   Herr Hamma, thank you for coming down so quickly to Berlin from Stuttgart. We have found a red Stradivarius of 1720. We thought you might be interested in purchasing it. My son and I have, of course, authenticated it, although we are concerned that there is no provenance.

HERR HAMMA   Prost!

[As he lifts a stein of beer]

It's a real pleasure to be with your son and you. I dropped everything to be with you two. I was excited to hear you might sell a red Stradivarius to me. Seriously, the lack of provenance is a concern. But go on, please.

RUDOLPH   Prost.

[As Rudolph lifts a stein of beer in return to Herr Hamma, Rembert lifts his stein too at the same time.]

Our initial research here in Berlin suggests this is the red violin The Mendelssohns owned over a hundred years ago. But. we have no proof, only a suspicion. The hundred-year gap in provenance is admittedly suspicious. Who owned the violin is a mystery. I agree with my son that the craftsmanship and the sound are those of a fine Stradivarius.[92] We have no doubt. It is in excellent condition, and the tone is superb. Antonio was at his greatest around 1720.

HERR HAMMA   How much do you want and will you take marks?

RUDOLPH   No marks, please. We will sell it to you for $3,500. That's a more than a fair price.

[Hamma picks up the violin, examines it for about 20 seconds shaking his head up and down, and then starts playing the Chaconne.

---

[92] How a Stradivari sounds depends upon the violin's condition, the bow being used to play, and how "sympatico" the musician is with the instrument.

After all, there is no repetitiveness in playing the Chaconne each time there is a pause in this play, because every great violinist, every great violin dealer, and every great theater attendee surely knows and loves Bach's Chaconne.]

HERR HAMMA   What a beautiful tone! Okay, I'll pay you $3,000. I know that's less, but I can't stop myself from bargaining. I've bargained all my life.[93] Perhaps, I can return your kindness someday if you accept. I trust your authentications, and I also agree it is a true Stradivarius. I can pay cash, write a check on an American account, or arrange a bank draft.

Rembert, what do you think?

REMBERT   I definitely agree it is a Stradivarius. The tone and craftsmanship are uniquely that of Stradivarius, and the Stradivari label is intact. The tone is breathtaking. The red color is beautiful. This is an absolutely superb, red Stradivarius of 1720 when the master was near

---

[93] Mr. Hamma doesn't ask immediately, "Why are you selling this violin to me at a bargain price?" He understands he is being indirectly bribed to be a better colleague to Wurlitzer than he is to W.H. Hill who was allegedly anti-Semetic anyway, as so many upper crust English were at that time. Hamma's acceptance of the violin at a bargain price is a slap in the face of W.H. Hill for having offered Rembert a job. Rudolph knew, of course, W.H. Hill would learn about the purchase. By selling the violin to Hamma, Rembert proved his loyalty to his father and Wurlitzer. If Rembert had not agreed to sell the violin, he would have failed the test of his faith in Wurlitzer.

his peak in his "golden period."[94] It's really a treasure.

HAMMA

By the way, why are you selling this violin to me at such a bargain price?

RUDOLPH

Done. A bank draft will be fine, and we accept your $3,000 offer. I'll give you a receipt of money and proof of sale right now. We are selling the violin to you because we need to pay our way back home to Cincinnati.[95]

[Rudolph writes out a receipt.]

You can take the violin with you.

HERR HAMMA

Prost,...

[As he lifts his stein of beer confirming the deal]

...und zum unser Bruderhaft! Prost, and to our brotherhood. It will be a bank draft that I will get for you before you leave. I can do this here in Berlin tomorrow. When do you leave?

---

[94] "The period from 1700 until the 1720s is often termed the 'golden period' of Stradivari production. Instruments made during this time are usually considered of a higher quality than his earlier instruments. Late-period instruments made from the late 1720s until his death in 1737 show signs of Stradivari's advancing age." Wikipedia.

[95] This representation is an obvious falsehood, but Hamma is too polite to challenge further.

RUDOLPH   Rembert and I leave tomorrow, late afternoon. We must get back home

HERR HAMMA   Great! I'll take the bank draft to the Hotel Adlon Kempinski. That's where you are staying? By the way, did you come to Berlin just to sell me this violin?

RUDOLPH   Yes, we're at the Adlon Kempinski, and no, I came primarily to make sure Rembert accepts a job offer we have made him that he's now accepted. He has proven his faith in Wurlitzer to me. We'll see you later tomorrow morning.

HERR HAMMA   It's been a pleasure.

[He lifts his stein of beer again, Rudolph and Rembert reciprocate by lifting their steins of beer. The deal is consummated by lifting beer to each other. It's good business drinking beer between reliable business associates.

Herr Hamma gets up, extends his right hand to shake hands with Rembert and Rudolph, and then departs.

A short time later after Herr Hamma has departed]

REMBERT   Dad, I will miss that violin very much. I played it every evening over the last two weeks. It's a glorious instrument. It became part of my soul. By God, I will buy it back from Herr Hamma if he ever sells it. I am afraid this violin has become part of me. I love that violin. I loved playing it.[96] I must possess it again. Most importantly, I trust I have proven my faith in Wurlitzer by having agreed to sell what was mine.[97]

Soliloquy #6

[Calmy and reflectively]

Ah, it just occurred to me. Possessing the violin might be a form of an Oedipus Complex where unconsciously, the violin I love represents my mother. I must possess the violin that is my mother again and again in order to displace you.[98] I must possess and then sell more Stradivari violins. I will become a serial possessor of rare violins.[99]

---

[96] Obviously, this is the sexual theme being inserted again.

[97] Many years later in 1949, Rembert forms his own company a year after his father died in 1948. The bond between father and son was finally broken then, but Rembert remained loyal to his father as long as his father lived. The memory of the violin he had sacrificed left a bitter hollowness in his soul, a lingering anger at his father. The love-hate relationship never died out completely.

[98] "In normal development, the male child wishes to possess the mother and eliminate the competitor for her affections, namely the father – i.e. the Oedipus Complex." Wikipedia

[99] Frequently in the cases of serial murderers, like Ted Bundy, there is a mother love-hate relationship that can lead to killing women reminding the killer of his mother. Rembert was not a serial killer. The author suggests Rembert suborned and solved his psychological conflicts by developing a strong need to possess and control rare violins. He became a serial dealer of Stradivari instruments.

Freud was right. There is an erotic connection to my fetish. I loved my mother very much. I remember now how much it disturbed me as a youngster when you kissed her. I wanted to possess her. I was jealous of you. I had repressed those thoughts until just this moment.

RUDOLPH I know Freud would agree with you. I'm pleased with your flash of insight. I didn't have to explain to you what I had already concluded. You will see *The Red Violin* again, I am sure. You will also see your mother again, I am sure too. And you will see many, many beautiful instruments again and again.

Herr Hamma promised he would reciprocate our kindness at some future time, and he is a man of honor. It's time, anyway, for you to recover from your Oedipal Complex and understand your psychological needs better. It's time for you to be a man. You don't have to be with your mother and the red violin every day. Have no doubt, there will be many many violins in your future. Hopefully, there will not be many, many women.

REMBERT That red violin is a mystery violin. It's in my soul. It's in my unconscious. It is a conflict in my mind to let it go, any more than I want to let my mother go. Selling it is like selling part of my soul or even my mother. I am getting no Faustian bargain in return. I feel no fulfillment without possessing it. But now I understand better why my life's mission will be to possess and control as many Stradivari and rare instruments as possible. My soul demands this commitment.

RUDOLPH

Relax, son. You'll recover. Time will give you other answers. I am pleased you finally understand yourself more psychologically. When you dreamt of possessing violins, you were actually dreaming of possessing your mother. Now, you can dream of possessing more violins, as rare as your mother. It's all right, son. You will recover and not have the same dreams. You now understand yourself better. You have already come a long way. You are no longer a lad.

SCENE #5

There has been a time-lapse of 30 years, and Rembert is back at the Berlin beer garden again, this time with Herr Hamma. Time has flown by so quickly that the café is still the same. Red lights, as if one were in a bordello, flash on and off announcing the opportunity for Rembert to buy the red violin he loves so much. The red color reminds him of illicit sex, and he suddenly remembers his morther again who has died. The year is 1956, and a sign outside says, "*Wir feiern 1956 mit Bier und eine feine rote Geige,*" and underneath, "We celebrate 1956 with beer and a fine red violin."

HERR HAMMA   Rembert, thank you for coming with your busy schedule back to Germany so quickly at my request. Your company is well known to all of us now in the violin business. You have accomplished a great deal. How many Stradivari violins have you purchased since I last saw you in 1926?

REMBERT   My Company has purchased, handled, or possessed over a hundred Stradivari violins since then. I am doing well. How are you doing?

HERR HAMMA   That is an astounding number of Stradivari violins to have possessed.[100] No one ever before can cite a number like that for handling

---

[100] Like Casanova who was the greatest seducer of all time called the "Michelangelo of Love," Rembert has pride in possessing many, many Stradivari. Casanova spoke of having had great sex many, many times with pride.

and selling Stradivari violins.[101] Casanova may not have possessed even that number of women.[102] Your record is most remarkable. Not even Luigi Tarisio or Baron Knoop owned as many Stradivari violins as you have. Most musicians don't believe that you have had so many great violins.

REMBERT   Thank you so much. I was not really a collector; I was a dealer. Most of the instruments I handled were on consignment. Others, sometimes, gave me credit for owning instruments I didn't own. But I did just buy *La Pucelle* last year.[103] Sometimes, I did buy fiddles.

Your English now is very good. If people don't believe what I have done, that is their problem. It's not my problem.

HERR HAMMA   Yes, for business I had to learn good English. Thank God I was not in East Berlin. The Russians are terrible. My city, Stuttgart, was heavily bombed, but not as bad as Dresden, thank God. Unfortunately, I must tell you we have gone through hell in this last war. We are

---

[101] This is probably an exaggeration. Other dealers like Hill, Bein of Hamma may have handled just as many or possibly more Stradivari. Hamma is stroking Rembert.

[102] Casanova allegedly seduced over a thousand women.

[103] As mentioned in an earlier footnote, Rembert bougth *La Pucelle* in 1955 according to Fulton Rembert stock records for $25,000. The Fulton Foundation sold the fiddle for twenty-two million in 2019.

still very much feeling the consequences. We have not fully recovered. Many of my friends and relatives died. I was fortunate to have survived. Businesses are still slowly recovering. The Marshall Plan has helped.

REMBERT   My father and I were always very fond of you. You helped us with many business deals. We sincerely wish the best for you and your family, and, of course, Germany.

HERR HAMMA   Thank you. Sadly, I need money now, and I want to sell the red violin to the man who authenticated it and sold it to me. Your father and you were exceedingly kind. I feel a moral obligation to sell it to you – if we agree on price. In fact, I feel obligated. So, I am giving you because of your help to me and your early involvement with this musical instrument masterpiece, a right of first refusal. You can buy it for a very reasonable price of $20,000. I believe once you have this violin, you will understand yourself better.

REMBERT   Herr Hamma, when you called me in New York and told me you wanted to sell *The Mendelssohn*, I was thrilled. I dropped everything to fly to West Berlin. Someday, we hope The Wall will come down. It's been a difficult time with East Germany being under the Russians and separate from West Germany. We can't even see or call our relatives in East

Germany. We have lost contact with relatives we love. Fortunately, we can still see our relatives in Vienna.

HERR HAMMA   Yes, it has been very difficult.

REMBERT   You are still a man who gets directly to the point and says without hesitation what he has on his mind. Thanks, too, for your sentiments. I am glad you are well, and I respect your directness and situation. In no way do I want to take advantage of you.

Yes, many of our relatives in Germany died during the war. The war was a tragic time for so many of those whose ancestry is German. We are blessed to be alive and Americans who have more than enough money to put beer and food on the table. Maybe someday, The Wall will come down, and we can see our relatives again in East Germany.

HERR HAMMA   *Gott sei Dank*. Thanks to God.

REMBERT

Soliloquy #7

[Again, related calmly]

Yes, God be thanked. I have always had a special fondness for the red violin that we now call *The Mendelssohn*. It is a magical violin. It is still a violin of mystery. It is a violin that I have dreamed about repeatedly for many years. Who owned it over the a hundred-year gap, we don't know.[104] We do not know its owners definitely. The Mendelssohns and the great violinist Joseph Joachim may have owned it.[105] We're not sure. It took years to research the provenance even while you were the owner. There is still a hundred-year gap in provenance. It is still a mystery violin. We didn't list in the Wurlitzer inventory as *The Mendelssohn* originally after I found it in Berlin in the late 1920s because we were not positive The Mendelssohns owned it. In fact, we didn't list it at all, because the violin was mine, personally. When I discovered it, I wasn't working for Wurlitzer.

How do we find documentation that doesn't exist? I don't know for sure if The Mendelssohns owned the violin. I really don't care.

I just want to buy it from you. I agree to the price of $20,000.[106] There will be no bargaining. I'll send you a bank draft. I'll live with the mystery and uncertainty. I just want to

---

[104] The a hundred-year gap is analogous to coitus interruptus. Unconsciously, Rembert saw many erotic connections.

[105] The Elizabeth Pitcairn web site (Elizabethpitcairn.com) lists Joachim as a previous owner.

[106] The author has no idea of the actual price; $20,000 is a reasonable guess.

possess the beauty of this violin. In my mind, there must be no more *coitus interruptus*.[107] I have felt a void in my soul for many years after being forced to sell the violin, my violin, to you in 1926. I will never sell it again.[108]

HERR HAMMA   For years, I sensed this conflict because of your constant questioning about the violin when we talked about other matters. It was obvious to me you missed it deeply. No bargaining? I'm a bit disappointed you didn't, although I was quite sure you wouldn't bargain.

By the way, your German is still very good. I will give you a handwritten receipt. Send me a bank draft later, and you can take the red violin now. *Auf Wiedersehen.*

REMBERT   Herr Hamma, please don't be in such a hurry to leave. Let's go out to dinner to celebrate. We have so much to be thankful for now.

HERR HAMMA   No, I have to go, and thanks for coming so quickly to Berlin. I have always enjoyed this beer garden since it was here that I bought the red violin from your Dad and you.

REMBERT

---

[107] "No more coitus interruptus," says Rembert can be inserted depending upon the director's tolerance for openness.

[108] There would have been no need to list the violin in inventory since he never intended to sell it. Hence, his stock cards do not show the fiddle's entry.

Soliloquy #8

It truly has been a privilege to have worked with you, and I am deeply grateful I can possess my red violin again. My soul is at peace again.

It is an honor to deal with someone based upon mutual respect and trust, without excessive paperwork and escrows. With your permission, I will take the violin with me. Be assured you will receive a bank draft soon. Then, send me a receipt. I will never sell my red Stradivarius. It is part of my psyche. I feel complete.[109] *Auf Wiedersehen*, unless I can take you out to dinner.

HERR HAMMA   There's no problem. Take the violin. I have no concerns about you sending a bank draft to me in Stuttgart. I'll give you a handwritten receipt right now.

[Hamma writes out a receipt while talking.]

Unfortunately, I have to catch the next train soon to Stuttgart and home. *Bis bald sehen.* I'll see you soon again, I hope, and I await your bank draft. *Gott sei Dank.*

REMBERT   *Gott sei Dank.* Thanks to God.

---

[109] The Id, Unconscious, and Superego are now reconciled.

POSSIBLE INTERMISSION

I would prefer there is an intermission, but I delegate that decision happily to the director. I don't like to make many decisions. This play is, I estimate, about 100 minutes long, so possibly it can be performed comfortably without an intermission, depending upon direction.

SCENE #6

It is now 1957 in Rembert's office in New York, a year after Rembert bought *The Mendelssohn* from Herr Hamma. He is talking with Francesco Mendelssohn, the grand nephew of Felix Mendelssohn.

FRANCESCO   Hello, Rembert. What a pleasure to see you again.

REMBERT   Yes, it has been several years since I learned that you had owned *The Mendelssohn* in 1913. But now that I own the fiddle, I still don't understand what happened between 1913 and 1926 when I found the fiddle again. A gypsy was playing it then.

FRANCESCO   It's a long story. Briefly, I've always had a problem with drinking. I have been such a clod. You may recall that one time in 1950 after a concert, I returned home on East 62nd Street absolutely stewed. I couldn't even enter my home. Then, in an alcoholic daze, I realized I was at the wrong house. I dumped my famous *Piatti Stradivarius Cello* on the ground, and found my house. I forgot about my cello.[110]

REMBERT   That's not funny. Well, actually it is funny.

FRANCESCO   I was so used to leaving my Stradivarius at bars to pay my drinking bills, I thought I had just

---

[110] Memoirs of a Stradivarius Piatti Cello. Jan 29, 2008. *Irish Times*. This episode has been well documented. https://www.irishtimes.com/culture/memoirs-of-a-stradivarius-1.932980 June 30, 2020.

left my fiddle at a bar where I had been earlier after the concert. The next morning, my housekeeper asked me if a cello she had found on the street was mine. She said trash people were about to pick it up, but she had grabbed it quickly.

REMBERT   What has that to do with *The Mendelssohn?*

FRANCESCO   Well, you may recall because a book has been written about my cello and me,[111] about the time I escaped from Nazi Germany on my bicycle going to Switzerland carrying my cello. If I had had *The Mendelssohn*, I would have taken it. It was more valuable than the *Piatti*. But I had lost *The Mendelssohn*.

REMBERT   You lost *The Mendelssohn*?

FRANCESCO   Yes, later in 1913 after I bought *The Mendelssohn* from Mr. Hammig,[112] I was really learning how to drink. After a concert and being thoroughly smashed, I left the fiddle on the sidewalk. Just as I would leave *The Piatti* in bars to ensure payment, I left it on the street to ensure payment to the trash collector.[113] The next morning, the trash

---

[111] *Adventures of a Cello* by Carlos Prieto. University of Texas Press.
[112] Fulton Provenance published in this book at the end of play references Hammig.
[113] So the near brush with violin death is great – suspenseful – but does one pay the trash collector or is service paid through taxes? The answer is simply Francesco was confused.

collector picked it up. He was pissed at me so he sold it to the gypsy you heard playing it in 1926.

REMBERT   You couldn't make up a story like that. Unbelievable. I remember the time you took a violin I made in Mirecourt rather than *The Piatti* on a trip. Then in a drunken stupor while smoking, you set the house on fire where you were staying. My violin burned up, but *The Piatti* was saved.

Truth is better than fiction. Sometimes, fiction is truth. You're entertaining, but dangerous to the health of musical instruments. It's fortunate I found *The Mendelssohn* in 1926. If you had kept it, you probably would have set it on fire or left it at a bar. Fortunately, you just lost it to a trash collector.

FRANCESCO   I'm grateful. You are true to my drunken heart.

You Rembert are "The Resurrector of *The Mendelssohn.*" I'm proud of you for discovering my lost soul.

SCENE #7

There is now a time warp. Whereas the last meeting at the Berlin café was in 1956 when Rembert bought the red violin, it is now earlier. It is 1953 in New York because the author suggests there be no shift of scenes. To go from Scenes #2 to #4 in Berlin to an office in New York as Scene #5, and then back again to the beer garden in Berlin would be awkward unless the theater has a revolving platform holding several scenes. Moreover, the author doubts Herr Hamma would have been willing to fly to New York to sell the violin to Rembert. When Rembert bought the red violin from Herr Hanna, the deal was almost certainly struck in Germany and logically at the beer garden where the author's father said the red violin was discovered. It was a practical decision on the author's part not to changes scenes back and forth to make it easier for the set designers and stagehands. Changing set designs unnecessarily would slow down the play. But if the director feels comfortable with quick changes in scenes, Scene #6 can become Scene #5, and vice versa. A revolving stage turntable with scenes would be wonderful. Then, the order of scenes could follow time.

The same office used in Scene #1 is appropriate with a few changes in decoration. This new venue is in an office at the Rembert Wurlitzer Company on 42nd Street in New York. The office is absolutely cluttered with books and rare violins. The year is 1953, and a sign on the side of Rembert's desk says surprisingly, "*Wir feiern 1953, indem Wir beim Geigenspiel Pabst Bier trinken.*" Immediately, under the sign, is the English translation, "We celebrate 1953 with Pabst beer while playing violins." Above this signage is a plaque that says, "Rembert Wurlitzer Company" and immediately below it, "New York." This scene is necessary in the author's mind in order to bring the young author into the play, and to stress Rembert's generosity.

Actually, this scene is not necessary and can be removed in its entirety by the director if he or she wishes to shorten the play. However, the author likes many of the soliloquies and would prefer the scene remains or at least many of the soliloquys that can be transposed elsewhere.

RAIMUND	It's good to see you again, Rembert. I have brought along my young son, Frederick, who is 16. He says he has an interest in violins.[114] Could you show him a Stradivarius, please?
REMBERT	Certainly, but let's talk. We need to catch up with each other. I was so sorry that after your father, Howard, died in 1928, you resigned from Wurlitzer. You had a great future with the company.
RAIMUND	Maybe so, although I was not sure what my father had thought about me. There was just too much going on. The Great Depression had an impact on me financially. Emotionally, I was very upset with my father's death. He was sick for thirteen years.[115] I felt the physicians could have done more. I wanted to do something new. My father freed me by dying. So, I moved away from Cincinnati out to California to become a stockbroker.
REMBERT	I hope you did well. How is your charming wife, Pauline? I understand her Dad, Fred Pabst, makes beer in Milwaukee. By

---

[114] The author visited Rembert with his father, Raimund, in New York several times.

[115] As told to the author by his father and confirmed by Lloyd Graham in Wurlitzer Family History 1942, it was probably a ruptured appendix. Before the age of antibiotics, not every patient who had a ruptured appendix died from peritonitis. Often, the ruptured appendix would cause a localized abscess leading to chronic illness. In a sense, the absence of the red violin from Rembert's life had lead to a chronic mental abscess with psychological disfunction for decades.

coincidence, I really like Pabst beer myself. I celebrate every day having a glass of beer.[116] I do this because my father used to say that one couldn't really trust anyone in business who didn't drink. I insist when I am doing a business deal that my customer and I drink a beer, unless he prefers another drink. I feel I can trust individuals more who drink than those who don't.

RAIMUND   My wife is fine. She's not with me now but will join me later in Cincinnati. She will be delighted to learn you like her father's beer. And how is your wife, Lee?

REMBERT   Lee is fine, thank you.

RAIMUND   Let's talk about violins. I understand that you are loaning the La Salle String Quartet four rare instruments for a concert my mother Helene is sponsoring soon on September 20, 1953 in Cincinnati.[117] It's in the news everywhere about your generosity. I wanted to thank you personally. I plan to be there myself to hear the

---

[116] The author does not know if Rembert drank a glass of beer every day. Marianne, Rembert's daughter had no comment. The author is taking literary license, but the author remembers Rembert served Pabst beer when Raimund and he visited Rembert.

[117]https://books.google.ca/books?id=18_CAwAAQBAJ&pg=PA110&lpg=PA110 &dq=sigmund+freud+and+wurlitzer&source=bl&ots=QPRZ8eaZWZ&sig= ACfU3U1_GQMzk39NWVXcsI-h4CAfgqCrg&hl=en&sa=X&ved=2ahUKEwjL8PvNz_XoAhXVu54KHbYE BO0Q6AEwFHoECBIQKQ#v=onepage&q=sigmund%20freud%20and%20 wurlitzer&f=false

concert and see my mother. You will be there, of course. Will Lee go?

REMBERT   I will be at the concert too, for sure. I'll be flying down from New York soon. Lee can't join me. We can have a beer together after the concert at the beer garden.[118]

It's true that I am loaning La Salle the *Baron Knoop* violin of 1715, The *Medici* viola of 1690, the *La Pucelle* violin of 1709, and The *Davidoff* cello of 1712.[119] I used to dream of *La Pucelle* or *The Virgin* while I was daydreaming about a girlfriend named Virginia.[120]

RAIMUND Someone suggested recently you don't own these instruments.[121]

---

[118] Mecklenburg Beer Garden was a favorite haunt for Wurlitzers

[119] From a private conversation with the grandson of Rudolph Henry, William Griess, whose parents attended the concert and kept a program.

[120] This interlude in 1953 was chosen because of the irrefutable evidence Rembert had *The Virgin* or *La Pucelle* under his control, despite Goodkind, Tarisio and others asserting Rembert was not associated in any way with the violin. Stradivari provenances are notoriously inaccurate. Mr. David Fulton has confirmed Rembert had *La Pucelle* on consignment in 1953 before buying it in 1955 for $15,000. Mr. Fulton's Foundation sold *La Pucelle* for $22,000,000 in 2019.

[121] Tarisio does not list Rembert as an owner of *La Pucelle*. Although Tarisio records are incomplete, *La Pucelle* was on consignment from Mr. Frank Otwell. That Rembert loaned *La Pucelle* to the La Salle String Quartet is well documented.

REMBERT

Soliloquy #9

That remark was partly true. I read it, and the reporter didn't even bother to contact me. Of course, I absolutely controled all four instruments. I had the *Davidoff* cello on consignment from Mrs. Strauss of Macy's. I plan to sell it to Jacqueline Du Pre with the help of Mr. Beare. The others I had on consignment. I would not loan them, and even less, put them at risk as luggage on a plane unless I took full responsibility. It was not practical to board with four very valuable instruments, so I was at risk. When I had instruments on consignment, I was working towards selling them for the owners. Because I took full responsibility at an agreed-upon price, consignments were, for me, like a form of ownership.

Yes, I know your mother is attending. It's sad my dad can't be with us since he died a few years back. We just haven't seen each other enough. I remember so well when we were together at that Berlin beer garden in 1926 when I found a red Stradivarius.

RAIMUND   When your father, Rudolph, died in 1948, I was upset. I was very fond of him. Truly, that time in Berlin in 1926 was memorable. What a remarkable story! I tell all my children about how you suspected a red violin was a Stradivarius initially from just the sound. Of course, you had to examine it to be certain. I am betting someday your story about a red violin will be made into a movie. Maybe, the movie will be called *The Red Violin*.

REMBERT   Thank you. I appreciate your kind thoughts.

RAIMUND   Getting back to the La Salle concert, it's grand you are making these brilliant temporary loans to their string quartet. You are being very generous. My mother is very pleased. I will indeed be at the concert, but I wanted to talk with you about another matter. You said you wanted to leave Wurlitzer because you didn't want to spend the rest of your life buying back Jay C. Freeman's mistakes. Could you tell me about that, please? I am quite curious.

REMBERT

Soliloquy #10

[A lot is being asked of the actor playing Rembert. A soliloquy here and there can be removed or interchanged with another soliloquy at the discretion of the director.]

Mr. Freeman's mistakes impaired the reputation of Wurlitzer, and they embarrassed me. His mistakes lead to questions sometimes whenever one intended to buy a violin with Mr.

Freeman's authentication. It was humiliating to have to buy back musical instruments whose pedigrees were truly not what Mr. Freeman had represented. This humiliation happened too many times for me to continue at Wurlitzer. I "didn't want to spend the rest of <my> life buying back Jay C. Freeman's mistakes."[122] But, I was not sure how my father would react. He had hired Mr. Freeman originally. I didn't want to offend my father, as I did when I dropped out of Princeton. My father and I have not always had a cordial relationship. Our love for each other was more like a love-hate relationship with each of us feeling ambivalence about the other. Simply put, because Mr. Freeman was my titular boss and had been appointed in 1919 by my father, I could not fire him. I felt I was in a vise again as I had felt being compelled by my father to go to Princeton. I felt my father had disinherited me by not promoting me over Mr. Freeman. I was angry.

RAIMUND   I recall you telling me years ago you felt like you were in a vise when your father demanded you go to Princeton. Truth be told, I had more or less a love-hate relationship with my father. He wanted me to stay with Wurlitzer when I

---

[122] direct quote from *Stradivari's Genius* by Toby Faber. Random House Paperback, New York. 2004. Page 194

had other ideas. I felt disinherited,[123] even as if he possessed me. My father also demanded I go to university when I didn't want to go. But I met my wife Pauline in university. So, university worked out for me.

REMBERT

Soliloquy #11

Yes, that love-hate relationship has been a central theme in our lives. Someday, we may explore the love-hate relationships our fathers had with their father, Franz Rudolph. This is not the time or place. I suspect love-hate relationships with the father are common among men.

I loved my father, but I hated his control over me. He treated me as if I was his chattel. Finally, I built up my courage to tell my father I wanted to leave. My father surprised me. He said he was pleased I wanted to leave. My wife Lee was enthusiastic too. Lee had been instrumental, pun intended, in pushing me to leave after becoming tired of my complaints. It seemed they all understood my psychological need to separate from Wurlitzer, like a boy becoming an adult separating from his mother.

---

[123] Raimund's mother did disinherit him ten years later in 1963, the year she died. Significant assets went to charities. The author intends to pass all his assets, if his wife is still not alive, on to charities.

RAIMUND	I had a similar relationship with my father. He controlled me. When he died, I rebelled by leaving Wurlitzer. I was finally free to leave. Did Rudolph help you financially?
REMBERT	No, I left Wurlitzer in 1949. My father died in 1948. He did not help me financially, although before he died, he had supported my decision. By 1949, I finally felt emotionally free to do what I had always wanted to do. I was finally alone with rare violins. I could possess them without owning them, without being monitored by my father.
RAIMUND	What a curious coincidence and how Freudian! After my father died in 1928, I left Wurlitzer the same year. That was two years after I was with you in Berlin when you identified a red Stradivarius. My father did not help me financially. That was one of the ways he controlled me. He did not want me to leave. His death freed me.
REMBERT	Yes, our fathers' deaths freed us. We have such curiously similar histories. Both our names start with "R." It's curious, too, that we are about the same age. You are about five years older, I understand.
RAIMUND	Several times over the years, you told me you sought beauty. What did you mean?

REMBERT   I feel like a poet being asked to explain a particular poem. I've sought beauty all my life. When I possessed Stradivari violins, I possessed beauty. There are Freudian connections my father told me.

RAIMUND   I'm not interested in Freudian connections. Sorry. How do you define beauty?

REMBERT

Soliloquy #12

[Many soliloquies can be interchanged.]

How do we define beauty? How do we define love? I do know that all Stradivari violins are works of art, but not all are works of beauty. Some are comparable to a Michelangelo sculpture or to the Last Supper by da Vinci. Like the Chaconne that has a beauty of musical structure, the best Stradivari violins are incomparable sculptures in wood that can produce glorious, breathtaking sounds. That is a musical synthesis. The ultimate mystery of how that can be leaves me bewildered with wonder. How is that synthesis possible? Even today, why Stradivari violins can have such beautiful sounds remains a mystery. Is it the "f" stops or mineralization? We don't really know. We still guess. It is a mystery how beautiful sounds can come from wood. Beauty is a mystery. Surely, God favored man with the beauty of red Stradivarius violins with particularly beautiful sounds. When I hear Jascha Heifetz play a Stradivarius[124] I feel the way he plays mirrors how I feel inside. That is beauty. In heaven, God ordains that his angels play the Chaconne only with red Stradivari violins like mine. Did you know that? That is true beauty.

RAIMUND   Our exchange has become intense. I appreciate it that you feel close enough to me to tell me your confidential feelings.

REMBERT   No problem. I loved my father, but I hated his domination of me. I compensated by seeking and possessing beauty.

RAIMUND   It's interesting we had the same problem of paternal domination. It was a central problem for the Wurlitzer founder whose father disinherited him.[125] Let's get back to my friend who is concerned about his violin purchase. He is considering purchasing an Amati from

---

[124] Actually, Heifitz played a 1742 Guarneri del Gesù. Rembert knew Heifetz who visited his New York shop multiple times. Nonetheless, Heifitz almost certainly played a Stradivarius Rembert had in stock. Where else would Jascha go to play several Stradivari violins except at Rembert's shop? Heifitz loved to play the Chaconne according to "God's Fiddler" Part 1 on *Youtube.com.*

[125] Raimund's mother Helene, the author's grandmother, disinherited Raimund years later. Disinheritance was a Wurlitzer theme. So was a love-hate relationship between father and son.

another dealer who questions Mr. Freeman's authentication.

REMBERT   Okay. You can trust my authentication or non-authentication of the Amati your friend wants to buy. The dealer cautioning your friend may be correct. Sometimes provenances remain a mystery and authentication difficult.

RAIMUND   My friend has the Amati on loan while evaluating it. I'll tell him to bring it to you. He is in California, but it would be worth his expense to fly to New York so you can look at it.

REMBERT   I look forward to that. What's his name, please?

RAIMUND   It's "John Smith." He wants to remain anonymous.

[There is an interruption, as a police officer after knocking on the door enters the room.]

POLICE OFFICER   Hello, Mr. Wurlitzer. Your secretary told me to knock and then enter. This is an urgent matter. We are detaining a man who had with him what we think a stolen violin. I have the violin with me. Can you identify the violin, please? Here it is.

[The officer hands over a violin. Rembert looks at the violin, turning it over several times.]

REMBERT   Yes, this violin is the three-hundred-year-old jeweled masterpiece Louis Amati made for King Louis XIV of France. I definitely recognize the violin. It was in my vaults, and then I sold it. I didn't know it was stolen, but I can definitely confirm the authenticity of this very valuable violin.[126] There is a scratch on the violin. I remember it. A forger would never have put on the exact scratch.

POLICE OFFICER   Thank you, Mr. Wurlitzer, for confirming the identity of this violin. I have to leave with the violin now. It was stolen. Thank you very much for your help.

[The police officer salutes Rembert and walks out.[127]]

RAIMUND   Does this happen very much? That was an unsettling interlude to see a police officer confront you.

REMBERT   No, this was the first time a police officer has come to my shop. But, I have authenticated other stolen violins like the *Ames Totenberg* Stradivari.[128] Many rare violins like the *Ex-*

---

[126] https://www.nytimes.com/1971/05/01/archives/a-stolen-amati-violin-is-found-after-5-years.html

[127] After WWII when the author's grandfather Fred Pabst hired German WWII veterans, they always saluted him or raised a hand to their chest as ancient Romans did. The author, as a small boy, found their salutes as to a superior military officer curious.

[128] https://tarisio.com/about-us/for-the-press/

Kym Stradivari were stolen. We now keep a stolen registry.[129] I have never knowingly sold a stolen violin. I do not operate a pawn shop. I am not a dealer in stolen violins.

Getting back to your friend, "Mr. Smith," are you sure his name is not "Mr. Jones"? I look forward to meeting Mr. Smith carrying a possible Amati violin. Hopefully, it was not stolen too.

RAIMUND   Do rare violins hold their value?

REMBERT   Over time, "Strad" and Amati violins increase in value. Historically, they have been very good investments. The Amati your friend wants to buy may be a good investment too, although I must examine it before making a recommendation.

RAIMUND   How do you identify violins?

REMBERT

Soliloquy #13

Pigment spectroscopic analysis and style can be important determining whether or not an old master painting is the "Real McCoy." If the pigment used in a painting is not the same as that of a master, the work is a forgery no matter

---

[129] Rembert's list of stolen violins is on page 40 of the Goodkind book.

how old the canvas may be. Sound analysis is like pigment analysis. It can point a finger at what is real. Today, we can use oscilloscopic wave analysis looking for specific Stradivari-like spikes in frequencies. I don't have an oscilloscope. I use my ears and rely on my memory for sounds. Most importantly, I examine an instrument carefully to see if the craftsmanship is consistent with that of the maker. I don't rely on just the sound. Sound is of secondary importance to physical examination. That's how I would confirm your friend's Amati is really an Amati.

RAIMUND   What about Carbon 14 dating or tree rings?

REMBERT   Yes, both can be used, but they're not usually exact enough. Most important are the craftsmanship and the provenance.

RAIMUND   But what about forgeries? Mr. Smith is concerned.

REMBERT

Soliloquy #14

I will tell you. Violins have been forged for generations. Violin forgery in the nineteenth century was a very busy industry for hundreds of luthiers. It was not always easy to tell a forgery.

Identifying Stradivari forgeries is neither easy nor a totally trustworthy skill any more than it is identifying old-master-painting forgeries. The Voller brothers made excellent forgeries.[130] The famous collector Jean Baptiste Vuillaume was also an excellent craftsman who made extremely excellent forgeries. On one well-cited and famous occasion, Paganini brought his Guarneri del Gesù *Il Cannone* to be repaired. Vuillaume made two copies so superb that Paganini could not immediately identify the original among the three instruments either by sound or appearance.

RAIMUND   Could you confirm a violin was a Stradivarius by sound alone?

REMBERT   No way! I never confirmed a violin was a Stradivarius by sound alone. Examination of the craftsmanship was essential. Even listening to the sound and examining craftsmanship could lead to mistakes, as Paganini found out when he examined his Guarneri del Gesù *Il Cannone* side by side with two Vuillaume forgeries. Vuillaume did what he did to sell violins he made. Customers wanted his forgeries.

---

[130] https://en.wikipedia.org/wiki/Voller_Brothers

RAIMUND	The Vuillaume forgery Paganini story is fascinating. I actually know it. Do you know of any other Vuillaume forgery stories?
REMBERT	Yes, I do. Many suspect that the most famous Stradivarius in the world, *The Messiah,* in the Ashmolean Museum of Art and Archaeology in Oxford is a Vuillaume forgery.[131] We know Vuillaume made copies of *The Messiah.* He was a compulsive, superb copier. His copies were incredible and are worth a lot today even as known fakes. But true Strads are well made and hard to forge. There are more forgeries of del Gesùs than Strads. I doubt *The Messiah* is a forgery.
RAIMUND	How often do dealers make mistakes?
REMBERT	We all made mistakes in authentication, but some dealers make more mistakes than others. After all, violin dealers are salespersons who, in order to make a sale, sometimes make spurious authentications. I never knowingly did that in order to make a sale. I felt my integrity was not just important to me personally; it was a strong selling point.
RAIMUND	Did your father and wife support you in leaving Wurlitzer?

---

[131] The "widespread speculation" may be grandstanding by Stuart Pollens.

REMBERT   Lee and Rudolph belatedly supported me very much in my leaving Wurlitzer. My father said, "Rembert, if you only knew how many years I have been waiting for you to come to this decision."[132] When Rudolph developed cancer and died in 1948, he had been unable to help me financially form my own company in 1949.[133]

RAIMUND   What else can you tell me?

REMBERT   One must be humble to be truly an expert, in my opinion. I was fortunate. God gifted me with perfect pitch and a really good ear and memory for sounds. I could identify forgeries much better than others occasionally first just from the sound, as I initially identified the red violin with you in Berlin years ago. But I need to stress sound is an unreliable test, because the condition of the Strad, the bow, and the player himself can impact the sound.

RAIMUND   I am still puzzled. How do you know the year a Stradivarius is made? You almost always refer to the year a Stradivarius was made. Is that the same for Amatis?

REMBERT

---

[132] From private correspondence April 2, 2020 with daughter Marianne.
[133] Private correspondence with Marianne Wurlitzer, daughter of Rembert.

Soliloquy #15

> That's really simple. All of the instruments that Antonio Stradivari made bore originally a label written in Latin that reads, "*Antonius Stradivarius Cremonensis Facibat Anno [date]*. The label indicated the maker, the place of production, and the date. Telling the year was simple unless the label was removed to put on a forgery. The best sounding Stradivari were made in the "Golden Period" from about 1710 to 1720. However, I could more or less also estimate the year by the craftsmanship even if the label had been removed to put on a fake copy. In many ways, I do not understand myself I could feel whether or not a so-called rare musical instrument was real or a forgery.

RAIMUND   Are labels reliable?

REMBERT

Soliloquy #16

> Labels can be misleading. Stradivaris and Amatis have labels that are often copies. What helps are certificates. Usually, they have a seal or a stamp. When I see a certificate with a seal that is recognizable with a signature I know from Beare, Hill, or Healey, I put a great deal of weight on what the certificate says.

Amati labels are usually inside the left-hand f-hole. Many labels can be faked, so it is important to compare the label of your violin against examples in their makers' archive. Making fake labels is simple; it is just a matter of copying a label and putting it in a violin. This has been done for hundreds of years. My job as an expert is to examine the violin carefully and make a judgment as to whether or not the violin is a fake. Sometimes, that is not easy.

RAIMUND Thank you for spending the time explaining all of this to me. What you've told me about forgeries is fascinating. It mirrors people we both know who pretend successfully to be what they aren't. Identifying the real person can take time.

What you have told me about yourself is far beyond what I expected. I consider you a good friend. That is more important to me than you and I being first cousins. I did not know the particulars about Mr. Freeman. I will tell Mr. Jones, Oh, I mean Mr. Smith, to seek your advice.

REMBERT

Soliloquy #16

It's buyer beware. All of us make mistakes. In a business like mine, forgeries are common and mistakes occur often. In life, we all make mistakes. As Alexander Pope said, "To err is human, to forgive divine."[134] Sometimes, mistakes are ignored and left uncorrected. I personally felt that it was my duty to be as honest and thorough as possible. That attitude was good for my business. It's an attitude that's good for any business and person. That's no mystery. I just made fewer mistakes than others, and when mistakes came to my attention, I always tried to correct them. That philosophy of correcting and forgiving error would help all of us socialize, even at a distance.[135] If people have a cold, tell them to stay at a distance.

RAIMUND   My father, Howard, was also as honest as he could be. Integrity is the most important trait when evaluating any major business.

REMBERT

Soliloquy #17

My authentications have value because of my integrity and their accurateness. I can live with myself in pride making true authentications. It was similar, I suppose, to the satisfaction some have confirming a woman is beautiful inside,

---

[134] This saying is from "An Essay on Criticism," by Alexander Pope.
[135] At the time of the author writing, the Coronavirus policy of social separation was in full effect.

not just outside. It may be a mystery, though why some people cheat by making forgeries and being untruthful, and others don't. The differences are not just because of money or greed. Identifying who a woman really is can be as difficult often as identifying a Vuillaume forgery. A common denominator in determining truth in a violin or in a person is looking for inconsistencies.

RAIMUND   It has been a pleasure and a privilege talking with you. As a cousin and a good friend, I will keep your confidences private. There are so many mysteries. What's real? What's false? As Pilate asked, "What's truth?" Why has our family maintained such great interest, now, for almost four-hundred years, in the music business? There is the mystery of who owned *The Mendelssohn*. There was the mystery too of what Stradivarius was it that you discovered years ago in Berlin. You found some evidence it had been owned by *Mendelssohn*s. Finally, there was the mystery of your love-hate relationship with your father and why it took so many years for you to leave him? I have been impacted by some of these same mysteries, especially the love-hate relationship with the father. Is that not curious?

REMBERT   Yes, there are always mysteries and themes that run through human existence. Some inconsistencies are never resolved. You, on the other hand, finally understood that the love-hate relationship you had with your father arose from envy of his relationship with your mother. That envy you had for your father may lead someday to your mother disinheriting you.[136] Your mother is very Prussian.[137] In her thinking, I suspect, a son never challenged the father.

It has been a pleasure talking with you openly. I can't do that with customers or even most family, including often my wife. *Auf Wiedersehen.*

RAIMUND   *Auf Wiedersehen.*

---

[136] Raimund's mother, Helene, disinherited her son leaving her very significant Wurlitzer estate including a fabulous art collection with Georia O'Keefes, Couses, Blumenscheins, and other Taos painters to charity.

[137] Helene Wurlitzer, the author's grandmother, was the granddaughter of a Prussian general. Her strictness was awesome. The author was afraid of her as a child. *Lady of the Casa* by John Skolle is a biography of her.

SCENE #8

More time has now passed, and it is now 1963, just seven years after the earlier visit of Rembert with Raimund in 1956 when Rembert bought the red violin. The Chaconne is played again softly and slowly as if for a funeral dirge. Red lights are dimmed briefly. Rembert just died, and his wife Lee is in mourning. She is in the office (essentially, the office in Scene #1 and #6) talking to a reporter. A sign on the wall says, "*Wir feiern nicht das Jahre 1963, das Jahr, in dem mein Mann starb.*" Underneath the sign in German, there is the English translation, "We do not celebrate this year when my husband died." Above this signage is a plaque saying, "Rembert Wurlitzer Co." and below it, "New York."

REPORTER	Thank you for meeting with me, Mrs. Wurlitzer. Your husband was a great man. He is sorely missed in the violin world. There has seldom been anyone like him who dealt with so many rare violins and who had the integrity he had when authenticating. I understand he or a Wurlitzer handled, repaired, authenticated and/or sold as dealer about 158 Stradivari violins.[138]
LEE	Yes, my husband was a marvel. He was kind, unusually bright, and extremely knowledgeable and intuitive about violins. His

---

[138] Actually, another Wurlitzer than Rembert or Rudolph sold a Stradivari. Marianne Wurlitzer, the daughter of Rembert, bought and then sold *The Maia Bang* Stradivari. David Fulton affirms there were 158 Strads that Rembert handled. My original list showed only 135 Strads for Wurlitzer and Rembert. Records and inventories of musical instruments are often unreliable.

memory was fantastic, and he could recount particulars about hundreds and hundreds of rare violins and thousands of musical instruments. His knowledge about rare musical instruments was encyclopedic.

REPORTER   But how many Stradivari violins did he possess? Frankly, reports that he handled and then sold maybe 158 Stradivari violins seem preposterous. Musicians I talk to don't believe the figures. Two musicians told me the 158 figure is ridiculous.

LEE   My Rembert was one of the world's greatest dealers ever of rare violins. He thought in terms of possessing them, if even only briefly, through consignment, rarely through purchase. As you mentioned, Rembert, together with his father, dealt with at least 158 Stradivari violins. Other Stradivaris were handled at the Wurlitzer Music Company differently where Rembert and his father Rudolph dealt with rare violins. The total number of Strads handled by a Wurlitzer was greater than 158. Many of these violins were also handled on consignment. However, many were purchased by Wurlitzer, held sometimes for months or years, and then sold. I've never seen a serial human relationship greater in number than the relationships my Rembert had with violins.

REPORTER	What did Mr. Goodkind think about the huge numbers of Stradivari violins Rembert handled?
LEE	Mr. Goodkind was fascinated with the numbers of violins Rembert had possessed. He facetiously referred to Rembert as the "Casanova of violins." Brief possession of violins was a fixation for Rembert. At the same time, he was never a womanizer, thank God.
REPORTER	Wow! I've never heard anyone before refer to Rembert as the "Casanova of violins."
LEE	Let's hope you don't. My remark is not to be quoted. Although the records do not show, while Rembert was head of purchases for Wurlitzer, whether it was Rudolph or Rembert who bought or dealt with a particular rare violin, the numbers cumulatively were impressive.
REPORTER	How did you keep track?
LEE	We kept "Black Books"[139] for violins we authenticated or dealt with peripherally. Our inventories were separate.

---

[139] Source was Marianne Wurlitzer, daughter of Rembert.

REPORTER   What about other great collectors? Were there any who matched your husband in the number of Stradivari violins handled?

LEE   Essentially, Rembert was primarily a dealer. He really didn't collect violins. He did buy violins occasionally, although most of the violins he handled were on consignment. Out of personal interest in answering your question, I did some recent research. Even Luigi Tarisio, a great collector and dealer, had just twenty-four Stradivari violins, and Alessandro Cozio Di Salabue, known as a supreme collector and dealer, had only ten. Baron Knoop had about the same number. Admittedly, my husband did not own all the Stradivari violins he handled at the same time, but, as a authenticator, restorer, dealer, and seller, he among a rare breed. There have been other dealers who may have handled as many or more violins than he, so let's not put too much importance on his numbers. Actually, Fernando Sacconi did most of our restoration work.[140]

REPORTER   Your allusion to Rembert as the "Casanova of violins" is provocative.

LEE   Many find Rembert's history of love for violins fascinating. Dr. Freud suggested to him once there were sexual connections. Freud told

---

[140] https://en.wikipedia.org/wiki/Simone_Fernando_Sacconi.

Rembert he had a fetish for violins. He even told Rembert later his fascination for *The Mendelssohn* could be explained as an Oedipal Complex. Rembert agreed with that analysis. His love for *The Mendelssohn* that he had found was like his love for his mother. He hid this illicit love by hiding *The Mendelssohn* and not listing it in his inventory.

> The real reason he did not list *The Mendelssohn* in his inventory was that for him it was a "keeper." Musical instruments in inventory were meant to be sold. *The Mendelssohn* was for Rembert a violin of great emotional importance. He never wanted to sell it. He would say to me the violin was part of his soul.

REPORTER   Did Rembert actually collect anything?

LEE   I would say he was a collector of pochettes, a few odd instruments such as a Quinton and bows, or other instruments with defects that were not particularly saleable.[141] *The Mendelssohn* was not part of any collection. It was like a wedding ring to him reminding him of his mission in life to possess beautiful musical instruments. Rembert saw *The Mendelssohn* as part of himself and much as his

---

[141] From private correspondence with Marianne Wurlitzer, daughter of Rembert.

hand was part of his body. His psychological connections to that fiddle were profound.

REPORTER   Did Rembert ever lie to you or to others?

LEE   Not to my knowledge. Like any human, he made mistakes. They weren't lies. He was a man of great integrity. A friend of ours with a sardonic sense of humor once said Rembert kept truthful track of his possessed violins with his stock cards as well as Casanova kept honest track of his conquests. That is a truthful parallel. My remark is not to be published.

REPORTER   What about records from other dealers?

LEE   Luigi Tarisio kept no records of any of his transactions, nor inventory of his collections. That is another reason why the Tarisio database is compromised. An estimated up to 1,100 instruments were made by Antonio Stradivari. Many Stradivaris are simply unaccounted for now, although they are known historically. More than a few owners hid or still deny ownership. Many Stradivaris were lost or damaged irreparably. There will probably never be a complete list of Stradivari instruments.[142]

---

[142] Goodkind, Herbert K. Violin Ionography of Antonio Stradivari 1972.

REPORTER   Does your company still retain the famous *Mendelssohn?*

LEE   *The Real Red Violin,* now called *The Mendelssohn,* was my husband's favorite violin from the day he first found it in Berlin around 1926. He gave it no name. Actually, Francesco Mendelssohn had owned the violin, but in a drunken stupor, he had left it on a sidewalk. Trash collectors picked it up and apparently sold it to a gypsy who played the violin at an outdoor café in Berlin where Rembert had been eating and drinking. His father Rudolph made him sell the violin to Mr. Hamma to consolidate relationships that were at risk. Later in 1956 Rembert bought his beloved red violin back from Mr. Hanna. He loved that violin like he had loved his mother. That love was possibly greater than his love for me. Yes, I still have that violin. But it is hidden. It is not even listed in our inventory. or in Mr. Goodkind's inventory that included our inventory.

Rembert won't even talk about the red violin with his children. There is just too much emotional overlay that he would find uncomfortable divulging to them.

REPORTER   What did the well-known Francesco von *Mendelssohn* say?

LEE	Francesco von *Mendelssohn*, who lived in New York, was a descendent of The Mendelssohns, He became a good friend of ours because Rembert had "resurrected" *The Mendelssohn*. In 1913, Francesco left the violin in a drunken stupor on a sidewalk. Trash collectors picked it up.
REPORTER	Are you saying one can love a violin?
LEE	Yes, indeed. There is no doubt that is true. Just ask famous violinists who play famous "Strads" if they love their violin. For that matter, ask violists who play famous violas if they love their instruments.[143] One might even say that a rare Strad can possess its owner. Rembert used to say he possessed *The Mendelssohn*, but sometimes I thought it possessed him. I am not sure he actually loved *The Mendelssohn* any more than Casanova loved his conquests. But have no doubt possessing his red violin kept his psychological needs for love at bay.
REPORTER	Is it unusual for a rare violin to disappear like *The Mendelssohn* did for almost a hundred years?
LEE	Stradivari violins disappear. Many that are historically known are not known now. Some

---

[143] A violist is someone who plays a viola. A violinist plays a violin. Frequently, musicians themselves are confused.

emerged later out of hiding like *The Sleeping Beauty* of 1704 that lay hidden within castle walls for generations.[144] Rembert resurrected *The Mendelssohn* that had been missing for about a hundred years. I've known wives who disappeared from their husbands for almost a hundred years.

Disappearance can be a survival technique for stolen violins and adulterous women. Disappearance can even work well for unruly husbands who fear their wives might kill them.[145]

REPORTER   What are you going to do with Rembert's company?

LEE   It's my company now, thank you. Now that my husband has died, I have taken over the company. I can say proudly that our company bought, sold, authenticated and/or restored more than half the world's six-hundred known Stradivari. Not all Strads were violins. We have supplied instruments to Fritz Kreisler, David Oistrakh, and Isaac Stern, among others. My company has a remarkable history. It would sell for a premium price, just based on the value of the brand name. "Wurlitzer" means music to

---

[144] https://tarisio.com/cozio-archive/cozio-carteggio/sleeping-beauty-stradivari/.
[145] The author's wife has told him many times when he became over the top that she would never divorce him. She would then reassure him she might murder him instead. The author assures the reader his wife was teasing.

millions of people. Nonetheless, I do not want to sell the company and its brand name. I do not want anyone to use ever again the name of my beloved Rembert Wurlitzer.

REPORTER   Do you have a buyer in mind?

LEE   Yes, and it may surprise you, that information is not confidential now. It's already been leaked throughout the music world. There is a music company named Moennig in Philadelphia. I am negotiating with them to buy our inventory of important, old, rare musical instruments. They would use their name, not the name of Rembert Wurlitzer in selling that inventory to musicians, not primarily to collectors.

REPORTER   What's in the inventory?

LEE   There are at least 1,400 objects including Guadagninis, Amatis, del Gesùs, Gaglianos, Roccas, Bergonzis, Stainers, Lorenzinis, Guarneris, and Giuseppes. Not all are on consignment.

REPORTER   What might the Wurlitzer collection be worth?

LEE   *[Lee laughs.]*

"Who knows? Until an old instrument actually changes hands, its value is unpredictable, especially   in   the   present   inflationary situation."[146] I'm not really that interested in getting the maximum amount possible or feasible. I want to sell our inventory at a reasonable price to a company like Moennig that would intend to sell the inventory to musicians. Selling to musicians may be, in fact, a condition for purchase in many cases where there are no consignment constraints.

REPORTER   So many Stradivari violins have odd names. Can you explain?

LEE   Many of the great Stradivari violins have engaging nicknames like *The Messiah, The Dolphin, The Virgin, The Lady Blunt, The Contessa, The Venus, The Sleeping Beauty*, and *The Molitor,* owned by Bonaparte. Nicknames have added to the magical allure of these magnificent instruments. A nickname gives a "halo of mystery" and a hint to provenance. It's a bit like provocative "Haloes of Mystery" given to famous women like "*The Daughter of a Whore*" for Elizabeth I; "*The Suffragist*" for Susan Anthony; "*Harriet, the S*lave," for Harriet Tubman; or "*The Notorious RGB*" for Ruth Ginsberg. Rembert thought of rare violins as beautiful, interesting women. He enjoyed possessing them briefly.

---

[146] Direct quotes from *The New York Times* Archives August 13, 1974, Page 26.

REPORTER	What about stories behind the great Stradivari violins? They are almost legendary.
LEE	Some Stradivari violins have amazing stories of being lost at sea like the *Red Diamond* of 1732 or the *Hartley* that went down with the Titanic and was later recovered. Others, like the *Sleeping Beauty* of 1704 or *The Mendelssohn* of 1720, were resurrected after many years. Stradivaris are often indeed instruments of mystery and legend.
REPORTER	What won't you do?
LEE	"I would never sell them at retail or auction them off, since that would mean that the collection, which has been insured for more than a decade at $1 million and includes some 1,400 "objects," would be gobbled up by collectors. I wouldn't want to see that. I want the instruments to be used by musicians."[147] Rembert was a good violinist. He wasn't really a collector. He didn't want to keep Stradivari instruments out of the hands of musicians. His father, Rudolph, had studied to be a concert violinist. Musicians were important to Rembert and me, especially excellent ones without sufficient money to buy a beautiful, rare instrument. A music company like Moennig

---

[147] Ibid.

would sell inventory to musicians, not collectors. That would be contractual. Maximizing what we might get would not be our prime incentive. I may even give a viola to my daughter Marianne who is a violist. I would definitely consider giving some instruments to excellent musicians who are not wealthy or even to charity.

REPORTER   Are you talking about the social issue of haves and have nots?

LEE   Yes, I am. We have an obligation to help others. That is not socialism. One can have love or not have it. When there is no love, a relationship can turn to hate. There was a love-hate relationship throughout Rembert's life with his father. With me, there was love and never hate, at least to my knowledge. Have and have-not relationships are not only about money. With Rembert, there was lust, almost a serial lust for beautiful violins, and in particular, *The Mendelssohn*. There was never hate. Maybe, there was never love.

REPORTER   What is the most valuable violin you own?

LEE   Perhaps the most valuable now on hand is the *Hellier* Strad, which was commissioned from Stradivari by an English family named

	Hellier.[148] It has had only three owners. It might be worth as much as $300,000. I may give this violin to a charity.[149]
REPORTER	Don't you have a son named Rudy? Isn't he interested in the family business?
LEE	He is a well-known writer. He's written screenplays and quite a few books.[150] He's not interested in running the business.
REPORTER	There are so many in your family named Rudy. How do you keep them apart?
LEE	It's difficult.
REPORTER	Wasn't there a Stradivarius that was lost at sea?
LEE	Some Stradivari violins have amazing stories of being lost at sea like the *Red Diamond* of 1732 or the *Hartley* that went down with the Titanic and was later recovered.
REPORTER	Okay, I will limit my further questioning, although surely you would like to say more in honor of your husband. I sincerely do not want to push you.

---

[148] https://www.nytimes.com/1974/08/13/archives/wurlitzer-to-shut-down-oldinstrument-concern.html

[149] *The Hellier* is with a charity in Cremona.

[150] Rudolph "Rudy" Wurlitzer (born January 3, 1937) is an American novelist and screenwriter. Wurlitzer's fiction also includes *Nog, Flats, Quake, Slow Fade, Drop Edge of Yonder*, and *Hard Travel to Sacred Places*. He is the son of Rembert. *Wikipedia*. Rudy was born the same year as the author.

LEE   One time, Francesco Mendelssohn told
                        Rembert facetiously he was the "Resurrector of
                        The Mendelssohn." I never called him that or
                        "The Casanova of Rare Violins."

REPORTER   What else would you like to tell me, please?
                        What do you feel when a Stradivarius is
                        played?

LEE   When one hears the Chaconne played well,

                        *[The Chaconne is softly playing again in the
                        background.]*

                        ...my heart trembles. When I hear the
                        Chaconne on a red Stradivarius, my heart
                        throbs. It is an emotional experience for me
                        when I hear a dazzling Stradivarius beautifully
                        playing gorgeous music. There may be no
                        greater beauty than hearing Bach's Chaconne
                        played beautifully on a beautiful red
                        Stradivarius.[151] For me, it is emotional. It is like
                        deep love in its intensity. Experiencing this
                        beauty is, well, excuse me, it's like beautiful
                        sex.

                        Rembert and his father, Rudolph Henry, who
                        studied to be a concert violinist, used to say
                        possessing and then playing a rare, beautiful
                        violin with gorgeous tones was like possessing
                        and having sex with a beautiful woman.

---

[151] Finally, we return to the central theme of beauty and seeking it.

Rembert used to call me sometimes, "my lovely violin."[152]

REPORTER   Aren't there other Stradivari made by relatives of Antonio?

LEE   Yes, indeed there are other Stradivari. Antonio's sons Omobono and Francesco made violins that are technically Stradivari violins, although their violins are not usually of the same quality as the violins their father made. Rembert or Wurlitzer handled nine of these other Stradivari that are included in the 135 number of Stradivaris Rembert or Wurlitzer handled.

[The Chaconne is played again for a full 30 seconds. Lee listens intently and reflectively, and then smiles.]

REPORTER   You seem lost in thought.

LEE   Yes, I was remembering my husband and his wisdom. Stradivari violins now sell for a million or more,[153] far more than what my husband ever paid. Rembert was a fine

---

[152] The author does not know this. He is using poetic license.

[153] A million dollars was a high price for a Stradivarius violin in 1963. In 2011, the *Lady Blunt* sold in an on-line auction for about $15,800,000. Now "Strads," if they come up for sale, sell routinely for millions. The Fulton Foundation sold La Pucelle in 2019 for twenty-two million dollars.

musician and an even better connoisseur of rare violins. He was a masterpiece himself.

My husband wanted to keep *The Mendelssohn* because it was the only Stradivarius violin he ever discovered. The red *Mendelssohn* brought back for him happy memories of sex and beauty. He talked in Freudian terms of possessing it. There is a qualified, private buyer who is unusually interested. I cannot discuss details.[154]

REPORTER   Is there any significance to the fact that *The Mendelssohn* is red?

LEE   Yes, the red color of *The Mendelssohn* is of significance. The red violin Rembert identified is not the only red Stradivarius known. The *Red Diamond* comes to my mind. Although most Stradivaris do not have a deep red color, those that do may have a more resonant sound than others not red. It may be because of a unique, red, mineral varnish that Antonio used from time-to-time or how the "f" stops were cut that created a beautiful tone. But keep in mind we

---

[154] Lee sold *The Mendelssohn* to Luther Rosenthal and Son after Rembert died for an undisclosed amount according to the Tarisio records of 40316 in 1990. That is obviously false, since Rembert died in 1963. The Tarisio database for an unnamed violin 51374 that is clearly *The Mendelssohn* represents that Rembert sold the red violin to Jacques Francais in 1968. Either way, the seller had to have been Lee. Take your pick as to the real date and the buyer.

did not categorize Stradivari violins according to color or specifically the color red.

REPORTER   Does red have any other significance?

LEE   The red color for a Strad can hold a special allure. Let me read you what the *Strad* wrote. I just happen to have a copy.

[There is another time warp since the Strad's September 2018 issue is being used. Lee pauses while putting on her glasses, and then reads.]

"The significance of red in our lives goes back to the Neanderthals, who buried their dead in red ochre. Every human culture has assigned some version of power to this color. In ancient China it was the color of health and prosperity. In the Arab world it signified divine favor and vitality. The Roman Empire was ruled by a class whose name, "coccinati," literally meant "those who wear red." It is the color of kings and queens, cardinals and demons."[155]

Red is the color of illicit sex. I often thought that Rembert saw sex in his red violin. Maybe, that is partly why possibly he never listed it in his inventory. Unconsciously he thought his love for violins was illicit, because his violin

---

[155] The magazine *Strad*'s September 2018 issue.

affairs were so brief. His affair with *The Mendelssohn* was not brief.

Although there are many Stradivari, those that are red are often truly special and seen as sexy, like *The Mendelssohn* of 1720, *The Red Diamond* of 1732 or *The Sassoon* of 1733.

REPORTER   Why do you want to sell? I've been afraid to ask that question. I really haven't wanted to offend you, and I apologize if I have.

LEE   I'm tired. I'm ready to retire. I want to smell the roses. I want to go to the theater. I want to just look at the Moon and drink wine while hearing the Chaconne and thinking of Rembert. I want to read naughty novels like *Delta of Venus* and *Lady Chatterly's Lover* again.

REPORTER   What's your most important memory?

LEE   That's an interesting question. All memories fade or disappear over time, but at least during the rest of my life, my love for Rembert will not in the least bit diminish. We had a three-way lust affair: for each other and for a red Stradivari violin. One observer commented that three-way relationship seemed incestuous.

REPORTER   Any final comments, please?

LEE   I am proud to have loved and supported my husband. I cry, knowing he died from a heart attack at such an early age of fifty-nine. I miss him terribly.

[Lee starts to cry, pauses briefly, then continues speaking while sniffling.]

I will do my best to run the company well, although we no longer have anyone with us that we can truly rely upon for authentications. We will liquidate over time. I certainly have no intentions of purchasing any instruments now. Neither my daughter nor my son wants to run the company. It's time for me to enjoy afternoon naps. I want to withdraw into my shell. Life has been good to me, giving me a fine daughter and son, and a wonderful husband. I'm not ready to die yet.

Thanks to God.

[As the lights dim, they turn a deep red while Chopin's Funeral March is played slowly, preferably on a violin or two violins rather than a piano, as a dirge.[156] A picture (seen below) of the deep red Stradivarius Mendelssohn *is shown on a screen. Then the dirge abruptly ends as Rembert's life abruptly ended with a heart attack.]*

---

[156] https://www.youtube.com/watch?v=1sJ8_d_ecTE This video has the Funeral March played on a violin.

Postscript

The Tarisio auction house lists Rembert as having bought *The Mendelssohn* (#40316) of 1720 in 1956. Tarisio lists Rembert as the first owner of another red (#51374) *Unnamed Stradivarius of 1720* or maybe some other name reflecting the original uncertainty that Rembert had found *The Mendelssohn*. The two violins listed by Tarisio are actually the same violin of the same date. The backs of both violins are exactly the same. The history of both violins was collated to give a history of the red violin Rembert never bothered to update his inventory to include *The Mendelssohn*. For Rembert, his red violin was a "keeper" not to be put in any inventory of musical instruments to be sold later.

The Mendelssohn was bought in 1990 by Mr. Pitcairn who gave it to his daughter, the famous violinist, Elizabeth Pitcairn. Mme. Pitcairn played her violin once, not that many years ago, in Sarasota, Florida, where the author and his wife, Ann, have a home.

Mme. Pitcairn is reported as saying she loves her violin and that it has given her life meaning by being her "most inspiring mentor and friend." Rembert might have made the same comments.

Records

Mr. Herbert Goodkind's book listing about 635 Stradivari violins[157] is the most authoritative source listing Stradivari violins. Rembert's daughter Marianne helped Mr. Goodkind with his recordations and memos. Rembert's inventory was given to Charles Beare in England, who, in turn, gave access to Mr. David Fulton, a collector in Seattle. Charles Beare had worked with Wurlitzer. His son Freddie is a dealer in England.

---

[157] Goodkind, Herbert. *Violin Iconography of Antonio Stradivari*. Self-published 1972.

This picture of the *Red Mendelssohn* can be shown on a screen as the lights finally dim in red, and then house lights are turned on.

Copies of the author's book, *The Real Red Violin,* can be made available at Intermission or after the play is over. All profits would go to the theater.

Provenance Presented by Mr. David Fulton.

Note from 1913 to 1990, the Fulton provenance is completely undeveloped. In the book and play, I develop the provenance for that time period. It is entertaining that, according to Mr. Fulton, Francesco Mendelssohn owned the violin in 1913. So, how did *The Mendelssohn* get from Francesco to Rembert? I suggest how in the Prologue and the play itself.

Violin

Antonio Stradivari
'Mendelssohn' 1720

BF S5684
RW
Hill

PROVENANCE		*Acquired through or from:*
		Notes on sources of info
1990	Elizabeth Pitcairn *	Christies
1913	Francesco Mendelssohn	
1913	Wilhelm Hermann Hammig	Bright
1901	Miss Bright	Kruse
1890.	Prof Johann Kruse	Riechers
1890	August Riechers	Van Hal
1879	M. Van Hal	Germain
1878	Emile Germain	Pinteville
1863	Baron Pinteville	Gand
186?	C. N. Eugene Gand	Darhan (with Wilmotte Strad)
18??	Sig. Bernardo Darhan	

BIBLIOGRAPHY   (* Illustrated)

2010   * Thone,
Jost; Antonius
Stradivarius 3 1990
    * Christie's;
Christie's Auction
Nov 1990

lot 360

1990   * The Strad Magazine Nov 1990

1972   * Goodkind, Herbert K.;   The Violin Iconography of Antonio Stradivari 1644-1737

1872   Gallay, Jules; Les
          Instruments des Ecoles
          Italiennes   Gand,
          Freddie Eugene;
          Stradivarius - Guarnerius
          Del Gesù
              as Pinteville; ex Garcia, ex Cadiz; 1879 Van Hal

Excerpts From Arthur F. Hill Diary

9/8/1891   Buziau also mentioned that one of the Strads. belonging to Mr. Vanhal, a professor at Brussels was bought in Paris for £160

3/9/1892   Kruser of Berlin, he tells me, has bought the Vanhals Strad. off Reichers for £1000.

5/2/1892   C. Fletcher called and expressed a wish to buy the Roberts Strad. He mentioned that he thought the Strad. which has just been bought by Johann Kruse through Reichers of Berlin from M. Vanhals of Brussels was paid for by Lord St. Seven.

10/17/1895 Lady Anne Blunt, in the course of conversation, said that a cutting had appeared in the Westminster Gazette this week relative to the value of a Strad violin. It was little puff which evidently emanated from Prof. Kruse [krause?] in which it is stated that his Strad violin was worth £1,250, and in which it is compared to Prof. Joachim's. This is a violin that has been offered to Alfred, and that three or four years ago belonged to Mr. Van Halls, and if I recollect the price he wanted for it was about £600. Riechers, the German dealer, who died not long ago, purchased it or negociated its sale but nothing like £1,250 was ever spoken of as its value.

10/29/1897 Alfred and I went to call on Professor Kruse, who has left Berlin to settle in London. He has very good rooms at 66 St. James'Street, and he evidently possesses means. We had quite a long talk, but at first I thought we should almost come to blows, as he tackled us over the general animus which he thinks we have against German fiddle makers. We showed him on what grounds we held these views, and told him many instances of their dreadful vandalism, and eventually he agreed with most of our remarks, and we parted very good friends. He showed me his Strad violin which is dated 1720. I have not seen it before, but I have often heard Alfred speak of it. It is a very fine type of Strad covered with a fine dark red varnish, and Kruse paid the sum of 22,000 Marks for it. Riechers, from whom he bought it, paid Mr. Va Hals of Brussels 19,000 Francs for it. However, he may have got it for less as Mr. Van Hals offered it to Alfred at a lower figure.

12/31/1897 Stradivari   Kruse   29 Oct 1897

4/1/1901 Professor Kruse brought us his Strad today for repairs. He wishes us to put a new neck. We are very chary about doing such work for great artists, although compliment is paid us by their asking us to do it. They are so fanciful and without rhyme or reason are often dissatisfied with the going of their instruments.

6/15/1913 Amongst various other items of news, we gleaned from him that Miss Wietrowetz is now playing on the

Stradivari which was formerly Kruse's, the Mendelssohns having bought this instrument and lent it to her, it was one which Kruse's favourite pupil, Miss Bright, the daughter of the late Jacob Bright MP, played on for many years.

REMARKS

This violin belonged to an amateur, Senor Bernardo Darhan. He was a pupil of Lafont and no doubt purchased the violin in Paris through his intermediary, he lived at Cadiz and retained the instrument for many years finally selling it together with a second example about 1860 - 65 to Gand freres for 7, 000 frs. Gand immediately passed one on to Wilmotte of Antwerp for 3, 500 frs. and retained the other subsequently disposing of it in 1863 to Baron Pinteville of Paris for 4200 frs. From the latter it passed 1878 to the hands of Germain (he paid 7500 frs.) who sold it to M. Van Hal of Brussels in 1879 for 14000 frs. In 1890 Riechers purchased it from the last named owner for 19000 frs. and resold it to Kruse for 12000 marks (£1100 this violin was lent for sometime by Van Hal to Hubay, the violinist. Sold by Kruse to Miss Bright for £1100 (K would not take a profit) about the autumn of 1901. Sold to Hammig of Berlin no doubt on the advice of Kruse 1913 - 14 and it is now owned by the Mendelsohns (I believe Franz M.)

PRESERVATION

excellent - belly underedged (done by Riechers of Berlin) a crack descends from top to bottom on right hand side, slight one at right top side - otherwise so far as I could discern sound. In character this instrument resembles the " Maurin Strad " - model rather flatter, head neat and the back has been trimmed away somewhat by a vandal. I note the right F is higher than the left.

DIMENSIONS

Length 14"

Width   8¼ - 6 and 5/8

Sides   1¼ - 1.3/16ths

WOOD

of back in two, broad wavy curl descending, sides, though plainer match - belly of open grain at flanks - head plain.

VARNISH

of plum red colour, the whole fairly well covered that on back picturesquely worn, it has been slightly retouched.

About the Author

Frederick Pabst Wurlitzer

The author, Frederick Pabst Wurlitzer, M.D., F.A.C.S. was born in San Francisco, although his four siblings were born in Cincinnati where the family business, The Wurlitzer Music Company, had been located. He was raised drinking Pabst beer while listening to Wurlitzer jukebox music.

Trained at Stanford, the University of Cincinnati, and UCLA, he did a later fellowship in surgical oncology at the University of Texas MD Anderson Hospital in Texas. For a brief stint, he was an Instructor in Surgery at U.S.C. Medical School in Los Angeles. Later, he practiced as an oncological surgeon, and he is still in old age a board-certified surgeon.

Although he has never published anything about Rembert Wurlitzer or The Wurlitzer Music Company before, he has written numerous medical articles published in over seven different medical journals, including the prestigious *Annals of Surgery, Vascular Surgery, Journal of the American Medical Association* (*JAMA*), *Journal of Pediatric Surgery, A.M.A. Archives of Surgery, Plastic and Reconstructive Surgery,* and the *Southern Medical Journal.* Not all medical publications are cited.

After retirement from active surgery in 1988, he volunteered numerous times for doing surgery, usually for a period of about two months each time, in Umtata, South Africa as a C-Section specialist, the Congo, St. Lucia, the Cook Islands as a surgeon for a nation, and about six months in Sierra Leone, West Africa, and elsewhere for a total of close to three years volunteering as a surgeon.

Pay was minimal, but psychological rewards great. Because usually there was no specialist care, he did orthopedics, urology, gynecology, and even occasionally thoracic surgery. Often in West Africa, he gave his own anesthesia.

His original intent on becoming a surgeon had been to work in Africa like Albert Schweitzer, a childhood hero. His short stint tours as a surgeon throughout the world reflected his affection for Albert Schweitzer and love for the poor.

Realizing that he had never worked in the U.S. for the indigent, he obtained a commission as a Commander (O-5) to work briefly in a Public Health hospital serving American Indian nations.

Politically, like most Canadians he is socially a progressive and financially a conservative. He votes as an Independent in the U.S.

He now lives most of the time in Victoria, BC, Canada with his Canadian wife, Ann, who was born in Quebec. They have known each other well for over 55 years.

He can be reached at franwurlit2@gmail.com.

Professional and other Publications (only a few of numerous medical publications are cited):

1. Wurlitzer FP, Ballantyne AJ: Reconstruction of the lower jaw area with a bipedicled delto-pectoral flap and a ticonium prosthesis. Plastic and Reconstructive Surg 1972;49:220-223

2. Wurlitzer FP, Wilson E.: Aorto-Pulmonary anastomoses using autologous pericardium. Vasc Surg 1972;6:128-132

3. Wurlitzer FP, Ayala A, Romsdahl: Extraosseous osteogenic sarcoma. Arch Surg 1972;105:691-695

4. Wurlitzer FP, Ayala A, McBride C.: The problems of diagnosing and treating infiltrating lipomas. Amer Surg 1972;39:240-243

5. Wurlitzer FP, Mares AJ, Isaacs H et al: Smooth muscle tumors of the stomach in childhood and adolescence. J Ped Surg 1973;8:421-427

6. Wurlitzer FP: Improved technique for radical transthoracic forequarter amputation. Annals Surg 1972;177:467-471

7. Wurlitzer FP: Volunteering in West Africa. West J Med 1991;154:730-732

8. Books by Fred Pabst Wurlitzer

- *The Gospel of Fred* – 2019
- *The Second Gospel of Fred* - 2019
- *Love to the Trinity* – 2020
- *The Real Red Violin* -- 2020